World's Series – Braves 5 Athletics 4 12 Innings Fenway Park American League Grounds Oct

REDSOX

BOSTON
1901 TO TODAY

A RETROSPECTIVE OF BOSTON BASEBALL

Edited by Ken Leiker, Alan Schwarz and Mark Vancil

STERLING PUBLISHING

NEW YORK

photo by
RILEY
55 Troy St
BOSTON MASS

Copyrighted

Published by Sterling Publishing Co., Inc.
387 Park Avenue South, New York, NY 10016

©2005 by Sterling Publishing Co., Inc.

Designed and Produced by: Rare Air Media
925 Green Bay Road., Suite 4, Winnetka, IL 60000

Distributed in Canada by Sterling Publishing
c/o Canadian Manda Group, 165 Dufferin Street
Toronto, Ontario M6K 3H6
Distributed in Great Britain by Chrysalis Books
64 Brewery Road, London N79NT, England
Distributed in Australia by Capricorn Link (Australia) Pty. Ltd.
P.O. Box 704, Windsor, NSW 2756, Australia

ISBN 1-4027-2796-8
Printed in China by Midas Printing International Ltd.
10 9 8 7 6 5 4 3 2 1

ACKNOWLEDGMENTS

History might have changed in the four years since we first created this book, but the contributions of all involved remain the same. In this update, many of the same people helped pull new material together and refine the older, including Ken Leiker, who remains the kind of person we all hope to be. But this update would not be complete without including the original thoughts about the people who helped make this project possible.

Indeed, style might lord over substance and conscious introspection often yields to conditioned response, but there remain instances when uncommon kindness and character push through the cultural clouds to shine for all to see. We talk about these people because they touch a part of us buried beneath the day-to-day business of life. When we think about them, there is a quality to our memory. In the end, they are people who warm the moments and smooth the bumps. For this stretch of track, they extended from Boston to Atlanta to Chicago to New York and points in between. They are:

Ken Leiker, a friend and colleague, whose talent and character are self-evident. He never wavered despite the most unreasonable request and never once answered a problem with anything other than a solution.

Not surprisingly, Alan Schwarz came to us from Ken. Like Ken, Alan's ability and professionalism is matched only by his desire to achieve perfection—on deadline. Much of this book was born in Alan's mind and its quality, particularly in the writing, is a direct result of his efforts.

Larry Cancrow and Debbie Matson are the kind of gentle souls we all might hope to become. Kind and considerate despite a challenging life of his own, Larry calmly guided us through Red Sox history while making us feel like a member of his family. Meanwhile, Debbie was simply as kind, warm and caring as anyone you could hope to meet at church, much less in business. Dick Bresciani plowed through page after page despite ringing phones, appointments and more than a quarter century full of memories. If Dick saw it, then he remembered details not even the combatants could hope to summon. Indeed, every person that touched this project on behalf of the Red Sox was nothing less than kind and giving, including Jeff Goldenberg and Rick Subrizio.

Steve Buckley and Jerry Crasnick are old friends whose ability and kindness were essential to this book. The work of Allen St. John was equally important and the late-inning efforts of Herb Crehan and David Scott closed some last-minute holes.

Among the many pleasures born of this process was working with Ken Shouler, whose persistence was of particular importance in the Title Years chapter.

Though we met and exchanged thoughts almost exclusively through email, Steve Marantz's efforts on the 1967 season and his take on the 2004 championship season were essential to the integrity of the entire project. He wrote with passion and grace, providing context to defining years in the lives of many New Englanders. On the design side, Nick DeCarlo answered the call once again amid the challenges of a changing life.

At Major League Baseball, Don Hintze remains a committed business partner and friend. The sports publishing business is better with Don as one of its leaders.

The fingerprints of Dave Durochik, who once again captained our initial photography search.

And as always, the support, love and gentleness of my wife, Laura, and our children—Alexandra, Samantha and Isabella Rose, whose beauty graced the world during the initial creation of this book, and Jonah, who arrived since—remain gifts beyond any expectation.

—Mark Vancil

THE BREARLEY COLLECTION

Dennis Brearley walked his guests up the stairs of his studio and offered his chair. No matter where you looked history seemed to look back in the form of the famous and infamous, but always from print of a beautiful photograph. The Brearley Collection is one of the great photography collections in all of sports, one that Dennis, Sr. and his family, particularly son Matt and wife Susan, make available to thousands of fans across the country through a catalog and retail shop at Boston's Faneuil Hall. But what they have is secondary to who they are. The Brearleys opened their studio and photo files at a moment's notice and worked all weekend to provide us with images necessary to complete this book. If you have never seen the Brearley Collection, go to Brearleycollection.com or visit the Brearley Collection shop at Faneuil Hall the next time you're in Boston. With any luck, you will have the pleasure of meeting one of the Brearleys along the way.

SPECIAL THANKS

David Durochik at Sportpics, Michael Bacino at Corbis, Prem Kalliat at Sports Illustrated, Elvis Brathwaite at AP/Wide World Photos, Mario Prosperino at AllSport, Bill Burdich at The Hall of Fame.

PHOTOGRAPHY

AP/Wide World Photos	101, 119, 108, 124, 137, 164, 165
Archive Photos	130
John Bazemore, *AP/WIDE WORLD*	76
Boston Red Sox	30
Paul Chiasson, *AP/WIDE WORLD*	80
Brearley Collection	45, 82, 168-169, 190, 191
Corbis	8, 11, 12, 13, 14, 15, 16-17, 18, 19, 20, 21, 48, 50, 51, 52, 56, 57, 58, 69, 85, 86, 87, 89, 91, 92, 96, 97, 98, 99, 100, 101, 103, 104, 105, 106, 107, 111, 112, 113, 114, 115, 116, 120, 121, 124, 125, 126, 129, 131, 132, 133, 134, 136, 138, 139, 140, 141, 143, 148, 150, 151, 153, 156, 157, 159, 161, 162, 164, 165, 169, 170, 173-81, 183, 184, 185, 188, 190, 191
James Drake, *SPORTS ILLUSTRATED*	51
Otto Greule, *ALLSPORT*	51, 55, 66
Hall Of Fame	24, 28, 29, 30, 31, 34, 144, 147, 149, 152, 153, 154, 159
Walter Iooss	1, 26, 27, 32, 33, 40, 41, 46, 49, 35, 51, 89, 91, 108, 109, 122
Walter Iooss, Jr., *SPORTS ILLUSTRATED*	51, 57, 95
Fred Kaplan, *SPORTS ILLUSTRATED*	54
Heinz Kluetmeier, *SPORTS ILLUSTRATED*	189
Phil Long, *AP/WIDE WORLD*	71
Doug Pensinger, *ALLSPORT*	77
Rich Pilling, *MAJOR LEAGUE BASEBALL*	41, 42, 43, 51, 62, 63
Art Rickerby, *TIMEPIX*	110, 123

John Riley, *AP/WIDE WORLD*	77
Herb Scharfman, *SPORTS ILLUSTRATED*	191
David Seelig, *ALLSPORT*	75
Sports Illustrated	72, 78-79
Rick Stewart, *ALLSPORT*	52
Winslow Townson, *AP/WIDE WORLD*	76
John Williamson, *MAJOR LEAGUE BASEBALL*	67
John Zimmerman, *SPORTS ILLUSTRATED*	171
PHOTO RESEARCH BY SPORTPICS:	
AP/Wide World Photos	51, 125, 174
Scott Boehm, *SPORTFOLIO*	74
David Durochik, *SPORTPICS*	4, 6-7, 39, 31, 32, 37, 38, 42, 43
Kathleen Economou	80-81
Ric Fogel, *SPORTFOLIO*	68, 84
Tony Inzerillo	82
Louis A. Raynor, *SPORTSCROME*	97
Bruce L. Schwartzman, *SPORTPICS*	192
Sports Imagery Inc.	76, 77
Transcendental Graphics	2-3, 32, 60, 84, 97, 135, 145, 146, 148, 155, 158, 172, 188, 190-192
Robert Tringali, *SPORTSCROME*	6-7, 26, 32, 36, 37, 73, 197
Ron Vesely, *SPORTPICS*	88, 92, 94, 192
Bryan Yablonsky, *SPORTSCROME*	72
Michael Zito, *SPORTSCROME*	70, 186

TABLE OF CONTENTS

The Championship Season

BREAKING THE CURSE, THE RED SOX WIN THE 2004 WORLD SERIES

1

A VOLCANO ERUPTS, RELEASING EONS OF PENT-UP ENERGY, SPEWING MOLTEN LAVA IN GOLDEN RIVERS AND LICKING HEAVEN WITH TONGUES OF FIRE AND SMOKE. WHEN RED SOX NATION ERUPTED AFTER 86 YEARS BETWEEN WORLD CHAMPIONSHIPS, IT WAS VOLCANIC. THE LONG WAIT ENDED ON OCTOBER 27, 2004, AT 11:40 P.M. THE NATION WAS DELIVERED UNTO DESPERATE, GIDDY, UNSPEAKABLE HAPPINESS.

CALLIN' OUT AROUND THE WORLD—FROM THE FENS TO BACK BAY TO BEACON HILL TO THE BANKS OF THE CHARLES RIVER, RED STATE TO BLUE AND ACROSS THE OCEANS, BAGHDAD TO JERUSALEM, GENERATION TO GENERATION, LIVING TO DEAD—ARE YOU READY FOR THIS?

THE SOX COULD NOT BE BEAT.

THE NATION DANCED AND SANG AND CELEBRATED ITS BELOVED "IDIOTS"— THE LABEL THE SOX PINNED ON THEMSELVES, DESCRIPTIVE OF A SCRUFFY PANACHE AND FREEWHEELING ECCENTRICITY. BUT IN TRUTH, THEY WEREN'T EVEN THAT SMART.

THEY WEREN'T SMART ENOUGH TO KNOW THAT TRAILING THE NEW YORK YANKEES IN THE AMERICAN LEAGUE CHAMPIONSHIP SERIES BY THREE GAMES TO NONE IS SUPPOSED TO BE "INSURMOUNTABLE." NOT SMART ENOUGH TO GIVE IN TO THE CRUSH OF HISTORY AND THE VOODOO OF AN IMAGINARY CURSE.

THE IDIOTS BELIEVED IN THEMSELVES EVEN WHEN REASON AND SUPERSTITION INSISTED THEY NOT. THEIR FAITH WAS AS STUBBORN AS THEIR VISION WAS CLEAR: A WORLD CHAMPIONSHIP FLAG FLYING OVER FENWAY PARK, FOR THE FIRST TIME SINCE 1918. IDIOTS RULE! SAY HEY KEVIN MILLAR: PASS THE JACK DANIEL'S.

his tale of desperate happiness is best understood by recalling Red Sox Nation's despair on the night of October 16, 2004. In ALCS Game Three, the Red Sox lost to the Yankees, 19-8, and were one game from elimination. Fans hooted and jeered before virtually deserting Fenway Park by the eighth inning.

It was the Nation's darkest hour, and like Great Britain during the early days of World War II, it needed a Winston Churchill to stiffen its resolve. Instead, it awoke on Sunday morning, October 17, to the carping surrender of the Boston media.

"For the 86th consecutive autumn the Red Sox are not going to win the World Series," wrote *Boston Globe* columnist Dan Shaughnessy. The Yankees' lead, according to Shaughnessy, was "insurmountable."

Another *Globe* columnist, Bob Ryan, wrote: "The Red Sox have laid a brontosaurus egg… They are down, 3-0…and in this sport, that is an official death sentence. Soon it will be over, and we will spend another dreary winter lamenting this and lamenting that."

Boston Herald columnist Tony Massarotti wrote: "They are doing more than just losing now. They are disgracing the game and embarrassing themselves, and they are doing a disservice to the paying customers who blindly and faithfully stream through their doors. Shame, shame, shame on the Red Sox."

History seemed to be mocking the Sox — still fresh was the memory of Aaron Boone's 11th-inning, walk-off home run for the Yankees in Game Seven of the 2003 ALCS. History tallied Yankees' pennant-clinching triumphs over the Sox in 1999, 1978 and 1949, as well, not to mention 26 Yankees world championships after the purchase of Babe Ruth from Sox owner Harry Frazee in 1920. History was the phantom 10th player — the mystical Curse of the Bambino — that the Sox never could defeat. Small wonder the cream of Boston sports media was curdled in knee-jerk rebuke.

And not only the media.

As Game Four moved into the late innings on the night of October 17, with the Yankees ahead, 4-3, the Nation's braintrust gathered in brooding silence at Fenway Park. Assembled were principal owner John Henry, chairman Tom Werner, CEO Larry Lucchino and 30-year-old GM Theo Epstein, baseball's boardroom whiz kid.

Charles Steinberg, the club's public relations specialist, broke the silence. "It's important that we not assess blame tonight," Steinberg said.

Henry shot Steinberg a look that was clear. The man whose fortune was made assessing risk in financial markets already had computed the bottom line. A year earlier Henry had pushed to jettison Grady Little, the Sox manager who had stuck with a fatigued Pedro Martinez

in Game Seven, enabling the Yankees to come back. If history was repeating — and with the Red Sox and Yankees didn't it always? — then first-year manager Terry Francona was in the crosshairs.

The hot-tempered Lucchino slapped a wall and began composing a concession speech. Only a miracle could save the Sox, and perhaps Francona.

But it would have to be a whopper — no major league baseball team had ever rallied from a 3-0 deficit. Yankees closer Mariano Rivera — among the greatest closers ever — was coming in for the ninth inning. It would have to be epic and legend, a miracle for the ages.

"For the 86th consecutive autumn the Red Sox are not going to win the World Series."

DAN SHAUGHNESSY, Boston Globe

"The Red Sox have laid a brontosaurus egg... They are down, 3-0... and in this sport, that is an official death sentence. Soon it will be over, and we will spend another dreary winter lamenting this and lamenting that."

BOB RYAN, Boston Globe

The ownership group of Henry, Lucchino and Werner took control early in 2002, ending nearly 70 years of management by the late Tom Yawkey and his estate. The trio's mandate, Henry proclaimed, was to win a World Series. "That's not my choice," Henry said, "it's my role, it's my obligation to New England."

Henry formerly had been a Yankees limited partner and had owned the Florida Marlins. Werner, a TV sitcom mogul (*Cosby, Roseanne*), had owned the San Diego Padres. Lucchino, who played basketball at Princeton with Bill Bradley, had run the Baltimore Orioles and the Padres.

Epstein, then 28, was the group's choice as GM. He grew up a mile from Fenway Park, played baseball at Brookline High, graduated from Yale and interned with the Padres under Lucchino. Epstein embodied the new order of OBP-fixated (on-base percentage) executives.

The new owners spiffed up the old ballpark, adding seats atop the Green Monster and the right-field roof, expanding concourses and creating a nightly street festival on Yawkey Way.

They also set about to build a championship team, with Epstein assisted by statistics guru Bill James. Of the 2004 World Series roster, only nine players predated the new owners: pitchers Pedro Martinez, Derek Lowe and Tim Wakefield; catchers Jason Varitek and Doug Mirabelli; outfielders Johnny Damon, Manny Ramirez and Trot Nixon; and backup third baseman Kevin Youkilis.

The rest of the squad was assembled by the new regimen. Reliever Alan Embree was acquired in June 2002. Reliever Mike Timlin, designated hitter David Ortiz, third baseman Bill Mueller, first baseman Kevin Millar and pitcher Bronson Arroyo were acquired after the 2002 season. Backup outfielder Gabe Kapler came on board in June 2003.

After the 2003 ALCS debacle, Epstein began to deal in earnest. He ate Thanksgiving dinner at the home of Arizona Diamondbacks big-game ace Curt Schilling and acquired him the next day in a trade for three pitchers. Schilling approved the deal after learning that Francona, his former manager with the Philadelphia Phillies, was a leading candidate for the vacant Boston position.

A couple of weeks later, the Sox signed closer Keith Foulke, formerly of the Oakland A's, as a free agent. To shore up the infield, they acquired second baseman Mark Bellhorn (trade with Colorado) and shortstop Pokey Reese (free agent).

Each move would prove crucial, but perhaps not as crucial as one that was thwarted.

For nearly six weeks after the 2003 season, the Sox pursued Texas Rangers All-Star shortstop Alex Rodriguez, at $25 million a year the

highest-paid player in baseball history. They sought Rodriguez because they had been unable to extend the contract of their own All-Star shortstop, Nomar Garciaparra, and because they were hoping to trade their eccentric $20-million-a-year left fielder, Ramirez.

When the A-Rod deal fell apart over money, it not only gave an opening to the Yankees, who snatched up Rodriguez, but also left Garciaparra, a two-time batting champion, feeling aggrieved, sullen and underpaid.

Long a favorite of the Nation, Garciaparra had not regained top form after a 2002 wrist injury. Claiming an injured Achilles tendon in spring training, he was in and out of the lineup — with limited power and range — as the Sox limped at a .500 pace from the end of April to the end of July.

On July 24, Garciaparra went 3-for-5 and led off the ninth inning with a double as the Sox beat the Yankees, 11-10, on a walk-off, two-run home run by Mueller off Rivera. Their comeback from a 9-4 deficit featured a bench-clearing brawl incited by Varitek shoving his mitt into A-Rod's face. The dramatic win was said to awaken the Sox from a three-month slumber. Epstein was not convinced.

On July 31, Epstein pulled the trigger on the biggest Sox deal since Frazee sold Ruth to the Yankees. Garciaparra went to the Chicago Cubs while the Sox acquired first baseman Doug Mientkiewicz from the Minnesota Twins and shortstop Orlando Cabrera from the Montreal Expos in a four-team, eight-player trade. In another deal, the Sox acquired base-stealing specialist Dave Roberts from the Los Angeles Dodgers.

Essentially, Epstein traded offense for defense and speed. Cabrera and Mientkiewicz would tighten the infield defense, and Roberts provided a new option on the bases.

But Garciaparra's departure shook the Nation to its core — children wearing No. 5 jerseys went to bed weeping. Epstein, barely removed from childhood himself, needed a sleeping pill to calm his nerves the night of the trade. "We did the trade for the right reasons, but there would have been hell to pay if it didn't work out," Epstein told the Globe.

Better days — and for Epstein, nights — were ahead. Prior to the deal, the Sox were 56-46. After it, they were 42-18, propelling them to second place in the AL East, a wild card playoff berth, and a window of opportunity.

ANAHEIM PITCHERS WERE NO MATCH FOR A SOX LINEUP THAT HAD FINISHED FIRST IN THE AMERICAN LEAGUE IN THE FOLLOWING CATEGORIES:

.472 SLUGGING PERCENTAGE

949 RUNS SCORED

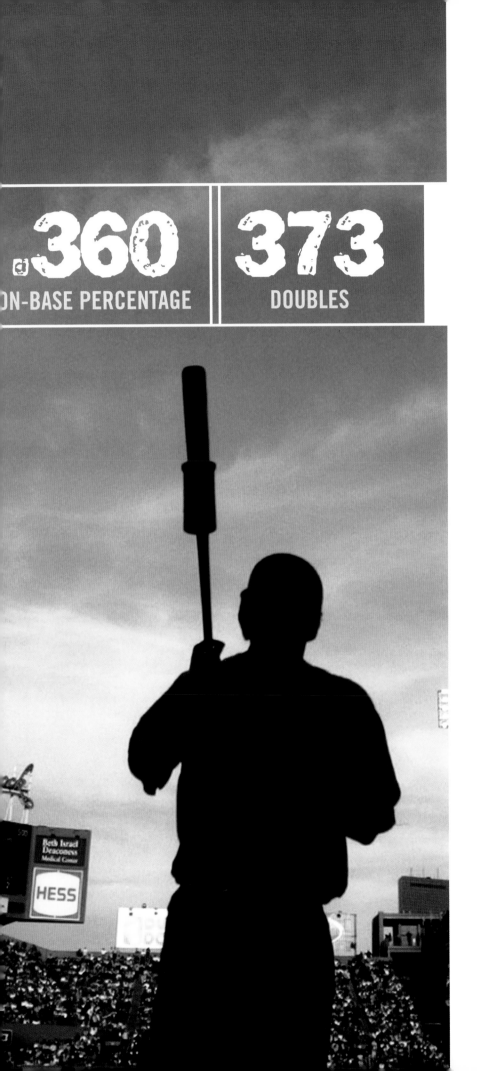

.360
ON-BASE PERCENTAGE

373
DOUBLES

D amon restated the team creed at the outset of the Red Sox's postseason division series against the Anaheim Angels. "We're just the idiots this year," he said. "We feel like we can win every game. We feel like we have to have fun — and I think that's why this team is liked by so many people out there."

With his Charles Manson/Jesus of Nazareth look, Damon was the club's iconic face and resident heartthrob. That he rode a Harley-Davidson to work — as did Millar and Foulke — added another layer of iconoclasm, much the way Nixon added layers of dirt and pine tar to his batting helmet.

While Damon had the longest hair and fullest beard, the hirsute median rivaled that of the Oakland A's of the early 1970s. Ramirez and Martinez could barely keep caps on over their unruly locks; Arroyo featured blond cornrows; Lowe favored an unkempt lumberjack look; Millar had the chin beard of an Amish farmer; and Ortiz's chinstrap growth was from a child's Etch A Sketch.

They weren't as clean-cut as George Steinbrenner's Yankees, but that was the last thing on their minds as the postseason began. They simply wanted to get to the Yankees — and Anaheim was in the way.

But not for long. The Angels went quietly in a first-round sweep. Just two years removed from their own World Series title, Anaheim shared a trait with all of Boston's eventual postseason opponents: a thin pitching rotation. Anaheim starters were no match for a Sox lineup that had finished first in the American League in slugging (.472), on-base percentage (.360), runs scored (949), doubles (373) and total bases (2,702).

The Sox blitzed the Angels by scores of 9-3, 8-3 and 8-6, with Ortiz staking his claim as the new *Señor Octubre*, hitting .545 and slamming a walk-off home run in the 10th inning of Game Three. Damon went 7-for-15, and Ramirez drove in seven runs.

The tea leaves were promising because of Martinez's seven-inning, six-hit, three-run effort in Game Two — after he had lost his final four decisions of the regular season. Martinez, a three-time Cy Young Award winner, had been so frustrated by the Yankees during a September loss that he uttered the most repeated quote of the season: "I can only tip my hat to the Yankees and call them my daddy."

Almost lost amid the optimism was the sight of Schilling massaging his right ankle after fielding a grounder in Game One.

"A tweak," Francona said.

The eternally bitter Sox-Yanks rivalry escalated after the Yanks won a 2002 bidding war for overrated Cuban pitcher, Jose Contreras. A frustrated Lucchino dubbed Boss Steinbrenner's club the "Evil Empire."

The fiercely contested 2003 ALCS — featuring Martinez's judo flip of rampaging 72-year-old Yankees coach Don Zimmer — elevated the rivalry above all others in American sports. Superstars such as Schilling, Rodriguez and outfielder Gary Sheffield wanted to be part of it. Sheffield joined the Yankees as a free agent prior to the 2004 season.

When the Yanks traded for Rodriguez — after the Sox fell short — John Henry complained that baseball's economic system was unfair and that the Yanks needed to be reined in. Steinbrenner deftly and publicly rebuked Henry.

After the Sox took six of seven games from the Yankees in April 2004, Steinbrenner told Sports Illustrated that Lucchino was "not a good man" and that he had "ruined" Padres owner John Moores and former Orioles owner Eli Jacobs.

At 74, Steinbrenner was the Lion in Winter. He had fainted at Otto Graham's funeral the previous December, his health was the subject of speculation, and he wanted another world championship — now. The Yankees hadn't given him one since 2000.

The Yanks ($183 million) and the Sox ($125 million) boasted baseball's largest payrolls. The Yankees had an All-Star caliber player at almost every position — led by indomitable shortstop Derek Jeter — and had won 101 games, finishing first in the AL East. In their division series, they whipped a solid Minnesota Twins club in four games.

Nonetheless, the Sox were favored to win the ALCS for two reasons: They had captured the season series between the teams, 11-9, and the Yankees pitching rotation was surprisingly mediocre.

While Epstein had landed Schilling the previous fall, Yanks GM Brian Cashman had reeled in Kevin Brown, an aging and brittle righthander, and Javier Vazquez, a gifted righthander nurtured in the isolation of Montreal. Both Brown and Vasquez washed out, leaving manager Joe Torre with Mike Mussina, Jon Lieber, Orlando Hernandez, a hope and a prayer.

A LCS Games Four, Five, Six and Seven stand alone as the dramatic centerpiece of the season. Before and after were mere prologue and epilogue — even the World Series was anticlimactic. When the history is told, those four games will be the epic poem — the Nation's Iliad and Lord of the Rings.

In the pantheon of heroes, Ortiz, who set Sox postseason records for walk-off hits, RBIs and slugging percentage, will reign a notch above Lowe, Schilling, Foulke, Wakefield, Bellhorn and Damon.

Millar, Mueller and Roberts will occupy a special alcove. A small pedestal is reserved for the Sox medical director, Dr. Bill Morgan, and Lady Luck.

Games Four and Five at Fenway Park exist as the *pièce de résistance*: 26 innings, 10 hours, 51 minutes of splendid baseball, tension, exhaustion, numbing cold (raw wind, drizzle, low 40s), and exhilaration.

When the history is told, those four games will be the epic poem —
RED SOX NATION'S ILIAD AND LORD OF THE RINGS.

Ortiz gave the Sox a 3-2 lead in Game Four with a two-out, two-run single in the fifth. Lowe, dropped from the rotation prior to the postseason, pitched a credible 5⅓ innings (six hits, three runs), and the bullpen shut out the Yankees for 6⅔ innings, with Foulke going 2⅔. The Yankees stranded 14 runners.

Still, the Sox trailed, 4-3, and would have been done — with Lucchino delivering a concession speech and Francona possibly out of a job — if not for the run they scored in the bottom of the ninth.

Millar worked Rivera for a leadoff walk. Francona sent in Roberts as a pinch runner and gave him a green light. On Rivera's first pitch to Mueller, Roberts stole second, just ahead of catcher Jorge Posada's throw. Mueller — whose walk-off homer had stunned Rivera in July — laced a single under Rivera's glove to center field, and Roberts dashed home.

Ortiz won it, 6-4, with a two-run, walk-off homer in the 12th. "We're down 3-1 right now, but you never know what can happen," Ortiz said. "We're going to continue trying to win. This is a team that never gives up."

Game Five was *déjà vu*, or in the words of Yankees manager Joe Torre, "Groundhog Day."

Ortiz's single off Mussina drove home the Sox's first run in the first inning, and in the eighth he cut the Yankees' lead to 4-3 with a massive home run off Tom Gordon. Varitek tied the game in the eighth with a sacrifice fly off Rivera.

Meanwhile, the Sox bullpen pitched eight scoreless innings, the final three by Wakefield, for whom poetic justice was rich, indeed. (Wakefield gave up Boone's historic home run in 2003.) Eighteen Yankees runners were left on base.

Ortiz won it in the 14th, 5-4, with a looping single to center off Esteban Loaiza that scored Damon, who had led off with a walk.

"I might be in sort of a haze, but I think that was one of the greatest games ever played, if not the greatest," Epstein said.

The series shifted back to Yankee Stadium, site of untold Red Sox nightmares. But the Band of Idiots was resurgent. In the clubhouse before Game Six, Millar passed a cup of Jack Daniel's whiskey and the players toasted themselves. In your eye, Boss.

Schilling took the mound with a temporary suture to hold down a loose tendon in his right ankle — the result of the "tweak" from the division series. The painful injury had cost him Game One, and until Morgan devised the clever fix, Schilling's season appeared over.

TV close-up views of Schilling's ankle revealed a blood-stained sock — marking the suture and his badge of courage. He pitched seven innings and held the once-potent Yankees — now demoralized — to four hits and a run. Rodriguez was called out on an interference play at first base — gaining him a measure of ignominy (more poetic justice) — and Foulke notched the save.

Bellhorn secured the 4-2 victory with an opposite-field, three-run homer off Lieber. Francona, criticized earlier for not benching Bellhorn — 4-for-31 in the postseason before his home run — was newly brilliant.

Game Seven — preceded once again by a Jack Daniel's toast — was practically over before it began. Ortiz slammed a two-run homer off Brown in the first inning. Damon followed with a grand slam in the second and a two-run homer in the fourth, both off Vasquez. Lowe, in command of his sinker, held the Yankees to one hit over six innings. Bellhorn added a solo home run in the 10-3 romp.

When Ruben Sierra grounded into the final out, the joyful scrum on the infield of the House that Ruth Built was a sight the Nation had longed to see and never will forget.

"We stuck together, and we erased history," Damon said.

Boss Steinbrenner, from behind closed doors, issued a statement congratulating the Sox, thanking his fans, and voicing personal "disappointment."

"You can be assured we will get to work and produce a great team next year," the statement read.

"WE STUCK TOGETHER, AND WE ERASED HISTORY."

JOHNNY DAMON

The Red Sox's World Series sweep of the St. Louis Cardinals was almost too easy. Winners of 105 regular season games, the Cardinals were flat and unresponsive after Bellhorn's eighth-inning home run beat them, 11-9, in Game One.

The Cardinals' vaunted sluggers — Albert Pujols, Scott Rolen and Jim Edmonds — went a combined 6-for-45 with one RBI.

Ramirez (7-for-17, 4 RBIs) was the Series MVP, but it could have been Schilling, Martinez, Lowe, Foulke or Bellhorn, as well.

Schilling stapled his ankle once more before winning Game Two, 6-2, aided by Varitek's two-run triple and Bellhorn's two-run double.

Martinez shut out the Cards for seven innings in Game Three, and Ramirez drove in two runs with a homer and single to key a 4-1 victory.

Lowe pitched seven scoreless innings in Game Four, winning 3-0. Damon homered, Nixon doubled in two runs, and Foulke closed out the game. Red Sox play-by-play broadcaster Joe Castiglione, voice electric, made the call:

"Swing and a ground ball, stabbed by Foulke. He has it. He underhands it to first. And the Boston Red Sox are the world champions. For the first time in 86 years, the Red Sox have won baseball's world championship. Can you believe it?"

As the world championship trophy was hoisted at Busch Stadium, Epstein said, "This is for anyone who ever played for the Red Sox, anyone who ever rooted for the Red Sox, anyone who has ever been to Fenway Park. This is bigger than the 25 players in this clubhouse. This is for all Red Sox Nation past and present."

As 2005 dawned, the Red Sox found themselves in a highly unfamiliar position: preparing to defend the World Series championship. The Red Sox had not operated under such circumstances since 1919, an era when it was easy to keep together a championship nucleus because players largely could change teams only on the whim of management. It's a different world now — players come and go according to their contractual status, and roster makeovers are an annual rite.

★★★ TITLE DEFENSE ★★★

Edgar Renteria was the only newcomer in the Red Sox's projected lineup for 2005. New to the pitching rotation were David Wells and Matt Clement.

★★★

THE LINEUP

C	JASON VARITEK	3B	BILL MUELLER	RF	TROT NIXON
1B	KEVIN MILLAR	SS	EDGAR RENTERIA	LF	MANNY RAMIREZ
2B	MARK BELLHORN	CF	JOHNNY DAMON	DH	DAVID ORTIZ

THE ROTATION

CURT SCHILLING	TIM WAKEFIELD
DAVID WELLS	BRONSON ARROYO
MATT CLEMENT	

It soon became apparent that not everyone the Red Sox wanted back was going to come back. Pedro Martinez, the Opening Day pitcher in each of his seven seasons with Boston, took a better deal from the New York Mets and sniped at the Red Sox and Curt Schilling on his way out the door. Martinez's work in 2004 wasn't up to the unusually high standards he had previously maintained, and Schilling, a shameless self-promoter but nevertheless a great pitcher and unyielding competitor, had slipped ahead of Pedro as the Red Sox's No. 1 starter. Martinez took it as a sign of disrespect that the Red Sox offered him the same money that Schilling was making and was outraged at the notion that anyone except him could be the No. 1 starter.

Along with Martinez, the Red Sox had to replace Derek Lowe in the pitching rotation. Lowe, despite his stellar pitching in the 2004 playoffs and World Series, wasn't offered a new contract. Schilling, too, would be missing at the outset of the 2005 season. He had soldiered through the postseason on a damaged and painful right ankle, and was still recovering from surgery.

The new pitchers came from the free-agent market. The Red Sox signed lefthander David Wells, who despite his portly physique and advanced age was still highly regarded and had a successful track record against the Yankees. The other significant addition was righthander Matt Clement, and the team also took a flyer on righthander Wade Miller, whose once-promising career had been stalled by a shoulder injury.

Among the everyday players whose contracts expired with the 2004 season, the top priority was catcher Jason Varitek, highly valued for both his skills and leadership. A catcher with such qualities could spark a bidding war for his services, but Varitek was adamant about remaining with the Red Sox and instructed his agent to strike a deal with the team. Along with a new contract, the Red Sox presented him with a red "C" on his uniform jersey as the team's third captain since 1923. (Carl Yastrzemski, 1966, 1969-1983; and Jim Rice, 1985-1989, were the others.)

The Red Sox would have been content with shortstop Orlando Cabrera, whom they had obtained in July 2004 in a trade that sent declining Nomar Garciaparra to the Chicago Cubs. Cabrera, though, signed with the Anaheim Angels, and the Red Sox were able to negotiate a deal with Edgar Renteria, the best shortstop on the market. Renteria already had a place in Red Sox lore. It was his bouncer to pitcher Keith Foulke — who tossed to first baseman Doug Mientkiewicz — that ended the first World Series in 86 years won by the Red Sox.

The Green Monster

THE MOST FAMOUS FENCE IN THE MAJORS

2

THE GREEN MONSTER

It is a movie screen of memories, a flat expanse towering over Fenway Park with decade upon decade of the grand old ballpark's charm and history projected onto it. Gaze at the Green Monster and then close your eyes — the plain background slowly morphs into images of Ted and Yaz and Dewey and Wade and Nomar, their swings and their gazes up to the Wall. The most famous fence in the major leagues — indeed, the most identifiable feature of any American sporting venue — might as well be a seashell, with its memories recorded inside and played back forever.

Every now and then when he played for the Red Sox, Nomar Garciaparra would walk out to the Wall before batting practice to see the history imprinted by countless line drives slamming against it over the years. "It looks like a golf ball — it has all these dents from all these balls hitting it," Garciaparra says with a boyish bounce. "When I see it, I think, 'I know I have a dent in there somewhere.' And you think of all the great players who have a dent. You look up there and it's a history of baseball. It's almost like a signature: Rice. Yastrzemski. A million names, all these great players. And I have one. Who am I next to? And who's next to me?"

Fenway Park, the oldest stadium in major league baseball, stands sentry over the sport's traditional past with its brick facade, obstructed-view seats and, more than anything, its unique outfield wall. Forced to conform to city streets and trolley lines as all stadiums once were, Fenway's fence has more nooks and crannies than an

English muffin — 17 faces in all, each with 17 dozen stories to tell about some poor outfielder bumbling around out there.

"It's not often that a center fielder can go straight to his left and slam into a wall," Paul Molitor says. For all its twists and turns, the best part of the fence is the 9,000 square feet of flat nothingness looming over left field. "I was always afraid," Bill Lee once said, "that it would fall down and kill Rico Petrocelli at short."

The Monster has been called dreamy by hitters, confounding by fielders, and words that can not be reprinted here by pitchers. John Updike called it "a compromise between Man's Euclidean determinations and Nature's beguiling irregularities." Even the distance of the Wall from home plate, once listed at 315 feet, is a mystery. A skeptical Boston Globe reporter sneaked into the park a few years ago, measured the distance, and claimed it was more like 305 feet. The official distance now reads 310. The Monster stands

"...a compromise between Man's Euclidean determinations and Nature's beguiling irregularities."

JOHN UPDIKE

WIDTH
231'

SCREEN
23'

HEIGHT
37'2"

FOUNDATION
22'

THE PROFILE OF A
GREEN MONSTER

37 feet, 2 inches high, and extends 231 feet long, its foundation sinking 22 feet below ground and its screen extending 23 feet above the wall — with the ubiquitous CITGO sign beyond it as the cherry on top. Seating for 274 was installed atop the Monster in time for the 2003 season, affording a fortunate few a whole new perspective of Fenway Park.

With baseball careening into the 21st century, tradition is vulnerable. Venerable old ballparks such as Tiger Stadium have been abandoned for modern, feature-filled facilities built for the contemporary industry. Fenway has survived, largely because the group that bought the Red Sox in 2002 has remained true to its promise to restore and enhance the old ballpark rather than replace it. After the 2003 season, seats were installed atop the roof in right field, and the owners planned to add another 2,000 seats after the 2005 season that would increase total capacity to about 40,000.

Whether the original Fenway remains or gives way to a modern version, the Wall is certain to survive, either replanted or replicated in the new place as a nod to the Red Sox's long history. And you can be sure it will continue to be painted the same Fenway Green presented by nearby Wilmington painter Ken Smith and approved by owner Tom Yawkey in 1947, and still provided today by his son John. "The Monster is the first thing people think of," Garciaparra says. "Even people who don't know baseball, when they hear of Fenway Park they go, 'Is that the one with the big green wall?' There's so much history here. I love it."

Fenway's left-field legend began the day the park was opened in April 1912. Though a 25-foot fence stood almost exactly where the Monster does today, the wall didn't capture people's attention as much as the precarious embankment in front of it. Known as "Duffy's Cliff," for Red Sox left fielder Duffy Lewis' mastery at negotiating the 10-foot incline, scurrying up and down it

SHERM FELLER

In Boston, there have been two voices louder than those of any other in the entire metropolitan area — nay, all of New England. This notion is as tried and true as Legal Seafood's New England Clam Chowder, Boston Baked Beans and The Tea Party, and will always and forever be so, with no room for discussion.

For the beloved Boston Celtics it was the gravelly, smoke-filled lungs of the late Johnny Most. And for Red Sox Nation, it was the deliberate, distinguished tones of the local institution, Sherm Feller. As the Boston Globe's Bob Ryan wrote after Feller's death in 1994 at the age of 75: "Central Casting just called. They regret to say they will not be sending over any more Sherm Fellers.

like a gloved gazelle, the embankment was as famous in its time as the Green Monster is today. Lewis, who would pinch-hit for a rookie named George Herman Ruth in Ruth's first game, July 11, 1914, succeeded where many others failed. A successor named Smead Jolley once tumbled down the embankment on his rear end and joked, "They taught me how to run up the cliff, but they never taught me how to run down it." It took less than a year for Duffy's Cliff to become, like the Wall did later, a part of Red Sox strategy. The Boston Post wrote during that first season:

If the Red Sox should win the pennant by a margin of two or three games — which is entirely possible — there will be no doubt that that bank made the difference....

It is sodded at an angle of forty-five degrees. To catch a ball running up this bank, or to run for one so that one can keep his equilibrium when he strikes the bank, requires study and practice.

When Lewis first saw the bank he realized that it was up to him to get the balls that went there, so he has practiced daily all season when the Red Sox were at home playing balls that are driven to the bank or against the fence. Nearly every game played at Fenway Park since then has given the spectators a chance to see Lewis dash for the bank, grab a fly ball in one hand and fall part way up the incline. Usually he lands on his back, but he always clings to the ball. It is a marvelous performance. It always brings applause. It usually prevents a score.

On the other hand, "the other fellow" cannot play the bank, and when a Sox hit goes out there it usually leads to a score....

The playing of this left field embankment is the most spectacular and athletic fielding achievement in either league. There is nothing like it anywhere else in the country. It is easy to see how, in a close pennant race, the ability to "play the Fenway Park bank" would be the deciding factor.

...He was the Count Basie of PA men. ...Sherman was a character with a Capital C, and we don't have many left in this town."

Not only was Feller one of the most distinct of the "old-time" public address announcers, the Army veteran was an accomplished entertainer, a songwriter and a composer, who wrote the hit tunes, "Summertime, Summertime," "It's Easter Time," and "She Was Five and He Was Ten."

Never one to follow a set pattern, Feller often lacked the precision of his counterparts but none could ever match his rhythm or his delivery: "Ladies and gentlemen... Boys and girls... Welcome to Fenway Park."

Brief at the microphone, Feller was a born storyteller away from it. As a disc jockey, Feller interviewed the giants in entertainment from Frank Sinatra to Nat King Cole to Tommy Dorsey, and was a fast friend to all of them. Many in show biz credit Feller with hosting America's first radio talk show.

However, it was the talking Feller did from the speakers at Fenway that brought him legendary status in Beantown.

★ FENWAY PARK ★
A TIMELINE

APRIL 20, 1912: Fenway Park officially opens.

MAY 8, 1926: The first Fenway fire occurs.

1931: The Red Sox players first wear numbers on their uniforms. The Red Sox have retired five uniform numbers: Ted Williams' No. 9, Joe Cronin's No. 4, Bobby Doerr's No. 1, Carl Yastrzemski's No. 8 and Carlton Fisk's No. 27.

JULY 3, 1932: The Red Sox play the team's first Sunday game at Fenway, a 13-2 loss to the Yankees. Sunday baseball was approved in Boston three years earlier, but not at Fenway due to its proximity to a church.

JANUARY 5, 1934: The second Fenway fire occurs.

APRIL 17, 1934: A newly rebuilt Fenway Park opens.

1936: A 23 foot tall screen is installed above the left field wall to protect the windows of buildings on Lansdowne Street, the road on the other side of the left field wall.

1940: Bullpens are constructed in front of the bleachers, replacing the old bullpen areas in the outfield foul territory beyond the dugouts.

JUNE 9, 1946: Ted Williams hits a monumental 502-foot home run to right field.

1947: Arc lights are installed at Fenway Park, making the Red Sox the third to last team among the then 16 major league clubs to do so.

OCTOBER 4, 1948: The first pennant playoff game in American League history takes place at Fenway.

OCTOBER 21, 1975: The first World Series night game occurs at Fenway Park.

1976: Fenway Park gets its first message board in center field.

OCTOBER 2, 1978: The first division-deciding playoff game in baseball history occurs at Fenway Park.

2003: Seating for 274 is installed on top of the Green Monster.

Thanks to Fenway's modern amenities (for that era) and the great teams that played there — the Red Sox won the World Series that first season and three of the following 13 years — Boston fans quickly forgot the old dilapidated park in which their team had played since joining the American League in 1901. The Huntington Avenue Grounds, less than a mile from Fenway Park, had spotty grass from its previous incarnation as a carnival site and a tool shed in deep center field. Nonetheless the wooden park played host to the first World Series, in 1903, when the Boston Pilgrims beat the Pittsburgh Pirates, five games to three, often with fans roped off beyond the outfield. Two Red Sox wins came via the right arm of Cy Young, whose statue now stands where the park once did, on the campus of Northeastern University.

Fenway played host to its first major league game on April 20, 1912, with Boston mayor John "Honey Fitz" Fitzgerald (the grandfather of President John Fitzgerald Kennedy) throwing out the ceremonial first pitch. News of the opening was pushed off the top of Boston's front pages by the sinking of the Titanic a few days earlier. The presence of the tall, wooden wall 315 feet down the left-field line wasn't particularly notable because that era's "dead ball" rarely traveled so far. When Hugh Bradley hit the first home run over the Wall, a local newspaper ran a cartoon with the caption, "It doesn't seem human!" While the Red Sox hit 29 home runs in 1912 (most in the American League), that total was six fewer than they had hit the previous year at the Huntington Grounds — a decline due largely to

"I ONLY WISH THE WALL WAS IN RIGHT FIELD."

CARL YASTRZEMSKI

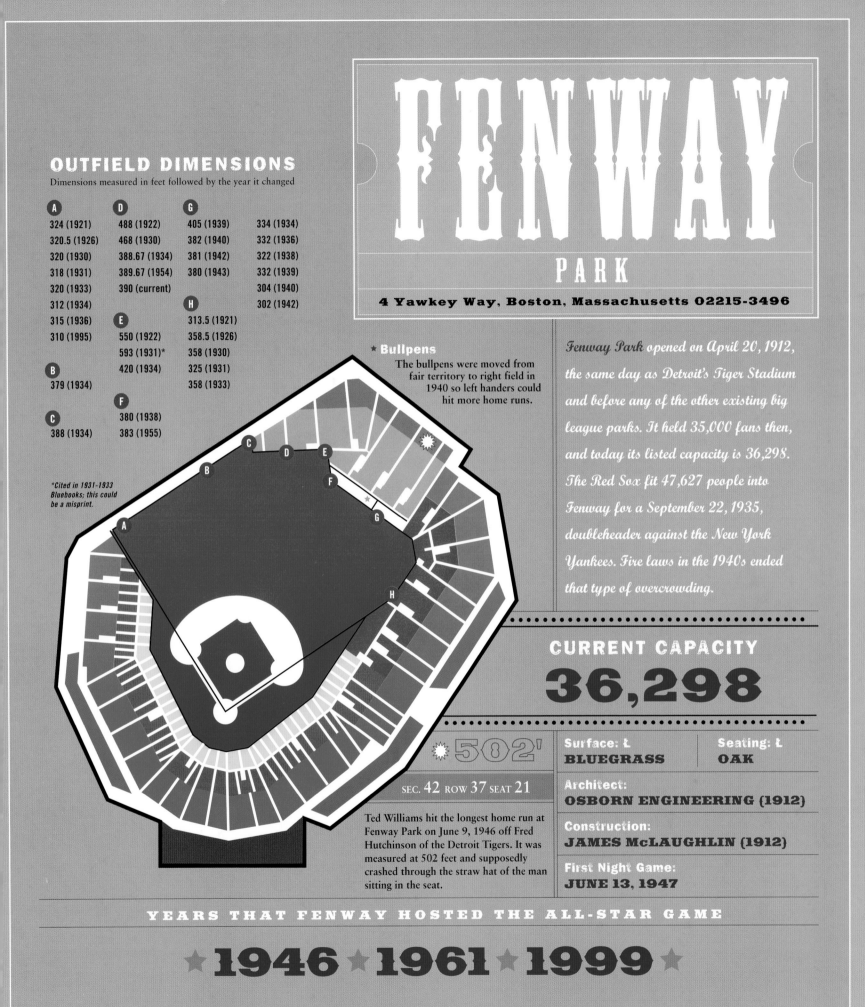

OUTFIELD DIMENSIONS

Dimensions measured in feet followed by the year it changed

A
324 (1921)
320.5 (1926)
320 (1930)
318 (1931)
320 (1933)
312 (1934)
315 (1936)
310 (1995)

B
379 (1934)

C
388 (1934)

D
488 (1922)
468 (1930)
388.67 (1934)
389.67 (1954)
390 (current)

E
550 (1922)
593 (1931)*
420 (1934)

F
380 (1938)
383 (1955)

G
405 (1939)
382 (1940)
381 (1942)
380 (1943)

H
313.5 (1921)
358.5 (1926)
358 (1930)
325 (1931)
358 (1933)

334 (1934)
332 (1936)
322 (1938)
332 (1939)
304 (1940)
302 (1942)

Cited in 1931-1933 Bluebooks; this could be a misprint.

★ **Bullpens**
The bullpens were moved from fair territory to right field in 1940 so left handers could hit more home runs.

FENWAY
PARK

4 Yawkey Way, Boston, Massachusetts 02215-3496

Fenway Park opened on April 20, 1912, the same day as Detroit's Tiger Stadium and before any of the other existing big league parks. It held 35,000 fans then, and today its listed capacity is 36,298. The Red Sox fit 47,627 people into Fenway for a September 22, 1935, doubleheader against the New York Yankees. Fire laws in the 1940s ended that type of overcrowding.

CURRENT CAPACITY
36,298

☀ 502'

SEC. 42 ROW 37 SEAT 21

Ted Williams hit the longest home run at Fenway Park on June 9, 1946 off Fred Hutchinson of the Detroit Tigers. It was measured at 502 feet and supposedly crashed through the straw hat of the man sitting in the seat.

Surface: ↳ BLUEGRASS	Seating: ↳ OAK

Architect:
OSBORN ENGINEERING (1912)

Construction:
JAMES McLAUGHLIN (1912)

First Night Game:
JUNE 13, 1947

YEARS THAT FENWAY HOSTED THE ALL-STAR GAME

★ 1946 ★ 1961 ★ 1999 ★

"Any ball down the line meant the shortstop had to come out. If it hit the tin, it dropped straight down; if it hit the cement, it would bounce back hard. If it hit a bolt, anything could happen."

TED WILLIAMS

Fenway's spacious center field, where the fence was 500 feet from home plate.

Penurious ownership led to Fenway deteriorating over the next 20 years, until the club was bought by Thomas A. Yawkey. The new owner sank $1 million Depression-era dollars into refurbishment for the 1934 season. Among many changes (like the leveling of Duffy's Cliff) was the first electric scoreboard, built into the left-field fence with red and green lights to denote balls and strikes. But what surrounded the scoreboard was a sight to behold — a 37-foot high fence extending from the foul pole to center field.

Tin advertising signs covered the fence completely, with immense messages from Calvert ("The Whiskey With the

Happy Blending"), Gem Singledge Blades and Lifebuoy. In 1947, the same year lights were installed at Fenway, the signs were removed and the wall was painted a distinctive, grassy color. The Green Monster was born.

Ever since, the Wall has been like a bullfighter's cape, dangling deliciously, tempting hitters to salivate and breathe fire through their nostrils — yet often getting the last laugh. The Wall's close proximity to the batter's box wasn't nearly as ridiculous as the Philadelphia Phillies' 281-foot fence at the Baker Bowl or the New York Giants' 258-foot chip shot at the Polo Grounds, but the Green Monster's sheer size made it irresistibly tempting to batters. Right-handed hitters thrived in Fenway; Rudy York, Bobby Doerr, Jimmie Foxx and

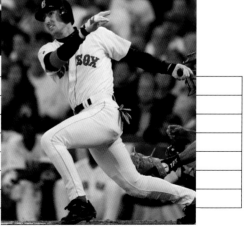

POS	NAME	AVG	GAMES	AB	H	HR
C	Jason Varitek	.299	420	1322	395	44
1B	Jimmie Foxx	.341	438	1606	548	126
2B	Bobby Doerr	.315	954	3554	1119	145
SS	Nomar Garciaparra	.332	498	2041	678	86
3B	Wade Boggs	.370	834	3067	1134	49
OF	Ted Williams	.361	1165	3887	1403	248
OF	Tris Speaker	.353	301	1095	387	4
OF	Fred Lynn	.350	412	1482	518	69

Top Red Sox hitters by position at Fenway Park

SOURCE: PETE PALMER   THROUGH 2004 SEASON

1938 to this country," Arthur once told the Boston Globe, "we didn't have any money and couldn't speak the language. We were only 13 years old. Two days after we got off the boat we had our first job, selling newspapers at Fenway Park. We could say just two words — 'two cents.' That's how much the newspaper cost."

In short time, the brothers began selling Sox pennants to commemorate the 1946 World Series. It was a time long before "licensing agreements" and "exclusivity deals" complicated the paraphernalia business. Adapting to those changing times, Twins grew into a national sports institution, with many of today's pro shops doing what the D'Angelos have been doing since the 1940s.

In addition to being a memorabilia maker and seller (the business now includes new generations of D'Angelos involved in the business) Arthur almost never misses a Sox game, enjoying a run that puts Cal Ripken to shame. All the while, as he watches the local nine, D'Angelo remains proof positive that two cents can go a long way if you couple that change with hard work and a dream.

Dom DiMaggio pounded the Wall with countless line drives. Vern Stephens drove in 159 runs in 1949, and the next year he and Walt Dropo each knocked in 144. Three decades later, in 1980, 5-foot-4 Freddie Patek of the California Angels hit three home runs over the Wall and a double that just missed becoming his fourth home run of the game.

Though Carl Yastrzemski lamented, "I only wish the wall was in right field," lefties did benefit, too. Said Ted Williams in his autobiography, *My Turn At Bat*: "Even though I didn't hit out that way, I always said to myself, if you swing a little late it won't be the worst thing in the world, because there's that short fence, the defense isn't there, and slices or balls hit late can still go out. So I didn't worry about hitting late, and

what did that do for me? It allowed me to develop the most valuable luxury a hitter can have: the ability to wait on the ball."

There were drawbacks, too. Though close to home plate, the Monster's height frustrated line-drive hitters. "The Wall ruined me," Foxx said. "I hit dozens of drives that would have been homers in any other park but they were only singles in Boston."

The Wall caused the Sox to rely too heavily on right-handed power. They traded away future Hall of Fame shortstop Pee Wee Reese because they felt he couldn't take advantage of the Wall. In 1949, the club went 61-16 at Fenway but 35-42 on the road. (Lefties rarely batted against lefties at home.) Some say the Monster chewed up and spit out George Scott, who hit 27

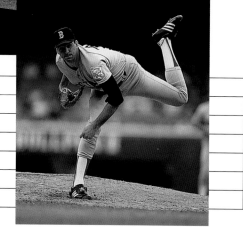

Top Red Sox pitchers at Fenway Park

NAME	THROWS	W	L	PCT.
Roger Clemens	R	95	55	.633
Mel Parnell	L	71	30	.703
Luis Tiant	R	69	36	.657
Joe Dobson	R	63	29	.685
Pedro Martinez	R	58	18	.763
Bob Stanley	R	58	43	.574
Tom Brewer	R	57	36	.613
Bruce Hurst	L	56	33	.629

SOURCE: PETE PALMER   THROUGH 2004 SEASON

homers as a rookie in 1966 then plummeted to 19 and three the following two seasons. Yawkey tried several times to buy out the Lansdowne Street liquor stores so he could move back the Wall but always ran into political problems.

Whatever damage the Wall does to hitters can't compare to the psychological trauma induced on the poor pitchers living in the Monster's shadow. "Think about the Wall?" Dave Morehead once asked. "You don't think about anything else." Bob Feller felt almost claustrophobic on the Fenway mound, and Lefty Gomez claimed the

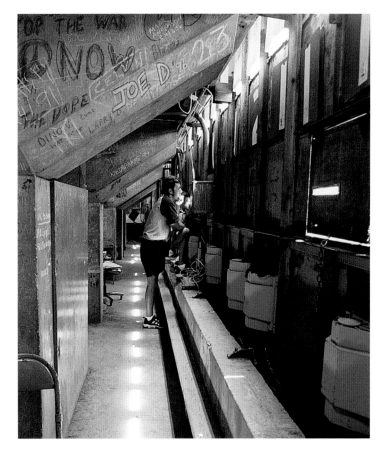

Wall gave him a heart attack. Said Bill Lee, "I felt like I was scraping my knuckles against it every time I went into my motion."

Some lefties did thrive in Fenway. Mel Parnell, who knew the trick (however difficult) was to pitch inside and lock up a hitter's arms, won 25 games in 1949 and 21 four years later. Lee, Lefty Grove and Bruce Hurst pitched effectively in Fenway. Today, pitchers are helped more than hurt by the park — after the addition of luxury boxes and the 600 Club level in the 1980s, wind patterns have changed to the point where the ball doesn't carry like it once did. This might have helped affect two of the weirdest developments in Red Sox history: No Boston outfielder hit 30 homers for 15 straight seasons, from 1985 through 1999, and in both 1999 and 2000, the team posted the lowest ERA in the American League.

Pitchers weren't the only players driven batty by the looming Wall. Said Yastrzemski in the book *Fenway Saved:* "If someone was trying to drive a left fielder nuts, this was just the way to do it." For 40 years the Wall was cement at the bottom and tin at the top; protruding bolts made for crazy bounces, as did the bulbs in the scoreboard; and pity the outfielder who watched helplessly as a ball caromed off the ladder that runs up all 37 feet. The Red Sox became synonymous with their left fielders — from Ruth to Williams to Yaz to Jim Rice to Manny Ramirez — in part because of the Wall behind them. Wrote Williams, "Any ball down the line meant the shortstop had to come out. If it hit the tin, it dropped straight down; if it hit the cement, it would bounce back hard. If it hit a bolt, anything could happen."

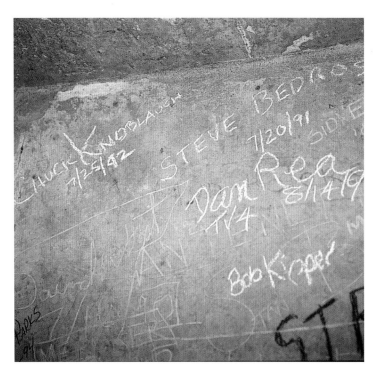

Yaz was unquestionably the best at playing the Wall to his advantage. When a fly ball was going to sail over his head, the seven-time Gold Glove winner wouldn't move — he'd pretend it was a routine pop-up, freezing the runners, or let the hitter think he had gone deep and slow into a jog. At the last second the ball would slam against the Monster, and Yaz would turn around, pick up the ball — having predicted the angle perfectly, often knowing the differences in the ball's spins off lefty or righty bats — and fire a strike to the right base.

The Monster got a facelift in 1976. The tin panels were replaced by fiberglass-like sheets that provided truer caroms — and less of a thunderclap when struck. The scoreboard also shrunk with the removal of National League scores. But the best job in the world remained: working the scoreboard during the game, being the person to slip in the 4 after a big Red Sox inning or crush the crowd with news of a far-off Yankees rally. Ted Williams used to talk with the scoreboard operators (usually local kids) between innings; visiting left fielder Lou Piniella would kick the wall to scare them. Their workplace is a 6- by 90-foot corridor behind the

Monster, a dank and musty crawlspace where they watch the action through one of six 1-by-9-inch slats. The corridor walls have become a three-dimensional autograph book. Dozens of players, from Jimmy Piersall to Mike Piazza, have signed their names on the concrete after venturing into the mouth of the Monster.

There are, indeed, creatures inside the Wall. One is almost solely responsible for changing the face of sports television. It was October 21, 1975, moments before Carlton Fisk's magical World Series home run. Camped out in the Green Monster to get shots looking in from left field, NBC cameraman Lou Gerard was supposed to follow any balls hit his way. But when Gerard spotted a large rat just as Fisk swung, in his moment of paralyzing panic he kept his camera on Fisk. The image that traveled through Gerard's lens and into 100 million living rooms will live forever: Fisk dropping his bat and madly motioning for the ball to land fair, bouncing on his toes while throwing his hands to the right, as if directing a jumbo jet on

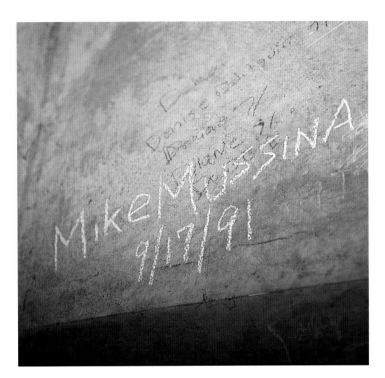

a runway. Seconds later Fisk leaped in glee, his home run ending what many consider the most exciting game of all time. "They didn't even know they had that shot," says John Filippelli, an associate director that night for NBC. "It was something like the sixth replay. It was a wonderful aberration that changed television. No one had ever thought of isolating on an individual." Ever since, directors have made sure to capture not just game action, but the emotion of the human beings who provide it.

It seems fitting that Fenway's influence will be felt forever. The Wall always has been about emotion — from frustrating pitchers to titillating hitters, from dazzling kids gazing for the first time at the old ballpark to providing old-timers the comfort that not everything has changed. The Green Monster is the largest tent stake in the world, resolutely securing baseball and Red Sox tradition as the hurricane of progress continues to blow throughout baseball. It is as textured as any flat surface ever has been.

The New Englanders

THE MEANING OF TONY CONIGLIARO

"Any Red Sox fan remembers Tony C—
if they're a fan."

THE MEANING OF TONY CONIGLIARO

The letters still arrive at the Conigliaro home in Nahant. Letters, flowers, testimonials…one woman once rang the bell solemnly and donated her scrapbooks. Richie Conigliaro can go to the supermarket, to the doctor, to a beach in Aruba, and at least once a day a stranger will recognize his surname, in a flash make the connection, and the memories cascade out.

"You're Tony's brother? Oh, man, he was my idol growing up in Boston."

"Tony was so special. It was such a shame when he got beaned."

"I can still see that home run he hit at Fenway…"

"He was so dreamy. Me and my girlfriends all had crushes on him."

"What an inspiration, the comeback and all."

"He was taken so soon. The poor guy…"

The emotions range from ecstasy to agony, because Tony Conigliaro means something different to every person he touched, which was most New Englanders. There is possessiveness to people's memories: Tony C was theirs. Still is. His story has attached itself to the gene structure of every Red Sox fan, inherited by succeeding generations like DNA and dimples.

They stargazed at the hometown teenager's rise from East Boston to Fenway Park in 1964, the boys marveling at his home run power and the girls melting before his teen-idol looks. They cheered as his clutch hits and dazzling defense helped make the Sox contenders again. They wept at the news of the frightful beaning that almost killed him and knocked him out of baseball for more than a year. They struggled with him during his comeback and exulted as he returned with (what else?) a home run in his first game. They cursed his unforgivable trade to California. They celebrated his second comeback with Boston following three years in retirement. And they agonized all over again when at age 37 a heart attack left this man, once brimming with personality and promise, to spend his final eight years unable to walk or speak, taking breaths as a mere formality. To live vicariously through Tony C — which a generation of fans did — meant continual swings from hope to heartbreak, not unlike being a Red Sox fan in the first place.

Tony Conigliaro was Boston's own, enjoying a fame and following even Ted Williams never did. Carl Yastrzemski never had it, either. However talented those two were, they remained somewhat outsiders, Williams from San Diego and Yaz from Long Island. Homegrown Red Sox are embraced with consanguinity unique to New England. The rest of the country abandoned Massachusetts at one point or another; the kids from families who stayed, the ones who played stickball and halfball with six inches of snow on the ground in November, always have been put on a separate mantel. Many have felt that love over the years — from Harry Agganis to Joe Morgan to Carlton Fisk. Yet none felt it more strongly than Tony Conigliaro did. "The Chosen One," as he was dubbed early in his baseball career, became everyone's brother, everyone's son, and everyone's tragedy.

"He carried himself like he was above us. By God, then he went out and proved it. He was better than us."

A CONIGLIARO TEAMMATE

Fans milling about Fenway Park on an April evening 26 years after he retired have stories at the ready. "He still carries that special image in people's hearts," says Jeff Boggier, a bank executive who was a Weymouth teenager during Tony C's heyday. "He was different. He was special. As a hometown boy he meant so much to local fans. We all followed him. It was like a cult. We don't put athletes on the same pedestal as we used to. It was more of a dreamy existence then." A fellow standing nearby adds, "Any Red Sox fan remembers Tony C — if they're a fan." Even those too young to have seen him play have been weaned on the Conigliaro legend. Says Sean Hicks, a 28-year-old Chelsean, "I hear his name everywhere. I think my mom had a thing for him. Women loved him; men wanted to be him. He was gonna be a Hall of Famer before he got beaned. I regret not having seen him play. I've seen tapes and read things, but it isn't the same." Hicks says one of his prized possessions is a Tony Conigliaro autographed baseball.

Parents named their children Tony, even Toni. Three Little League fields bear his name. Radio talk shows still crackle with listeners' memories. "Every kid my age wanted to be Tony C," one says. Recalling Conigliaro's fanciful foray into cutting teeny-bopper records in the mid-1960s, another says, "I remember this record

CARL YASTRZEMSKI, REGGIE SMITH, TONY CONIGLIARO

signing Tony had at Fullerton Chevrolet in Winthrop. It was as if the Beatles were there. There were lines as far as the eye could see. Girls screaming everywhere. It was just incredible. He really was a monster on the Boston scene. We really miss him."

Like most hurricanes, he blew both in and out with startling suddenness. The Boston Record-American reported early in 1964 spring training, "Rookie May Crack Sox Outfield," and before long this teenager from Eastie would be branded on the memories of a generation. Tony C.

He hit a home run on the first pitch he saw at Fenway Park, and proceeded to slam 100 home runs faster than any American League player before or since. He dated sex siren Mamie Van Doren. He careened into bleachers after fly balls. He sang on Merv Griffin's TV show.

There seem to be two kinds of athletic heroes: those who keep their head down in humility, and those who keep their head up, bursting with a fantasia of confidence and charisma. When during his first spring training Ted Williams offered him a Cadillac if he caught a tough fly ball, Tony C replied, "I already have a Cadillac." He strutted through his competition at 1964 spring training. As one teammate recalled in David Cataneo's fine biography, *Tony C*, "He carried himself like he was above us. By God, then he went out and proved it. He was better than us."

"It was as if the Beatles were there. There were lines as far as the eye could see. Girls screaming everywhere. It was just incredible. He really was a rooster on the Boston scene. We really miss him."

To New Englanders, he was one of them. Born on January 7, 1945, Anthony Richard Conigliaro spent most of his childhood in East Boston, 15 minutes from Fenway Park, his upbringing as idyllic as it was identifiable. Strict but encouraging father Sal; loving, lasagna-at-the-ready mother Teresa; Catholic school education. "The only 'A' I ever got on my report card was A. Conigliaro," joked Tony, who preferred stealing his mother's broom handles to play stickball and halfball until his hands bled. A local legend from Little League on, Conigliaro signed with the Red Sox for a $22,000 bonus out of St. Mary's High School in Lynn. He launched his pro career by hitting .363 with 24 home runs and 74 RBIs in 83 games and winning MVP honors in the New York-Penn League. Attending spring training with major leaguers only a few months after turning 19, he doubled three times in his first start. News flowed from Scottsdale, Arizona, back to Boston that a hometown teenager could open the season with the Sox; 25 letters a day flowed back from fans to Tony C with good wishes, and one marriage proposal — from a 12-year-old girl. As camp wound down, manager Johnny Pesky had little choice but to start the slugging phenom in center field come Opening Day: "Do you want me to get shot by the fans back home?" he asked. "Yes, Tony will be in there."

Hitting a home run in his first Fenway Park at-bat launched Conigliaro into stardom. Fans mobbed his car for autographs after the game. The Sox had been a mediocre bunch in the early 1960s, but the torpor lifted thanks to a kid who still lived at home, eating his mother's breakfast of juice, cereal, bananas and strawberries every morning. By this time, the Conigliaros had moved 10 miles north to Swampscott, sparking a tug-of-war between Eastie and the town that sports writers mistakenly said the new hero was from. "Swampscott Claim Resented," declared a headline in the Boston Globe. An East Boston liquor store owner, who displayed a picture of Tony C in a Red Sox uniform in his window, told the paper, "The kid is our boy. He's from up on the hill, Crestway Road. We all watched him growing up playing ball." Another Eastie native, identified as Francis "The Fastman" Valenti, said, "He's traveled most of his life on an East Boston passport. It's the fatherland."

The Pride of

NEW ENGLAND

CARLTON FISK

MIKE RYAN

BILL MONBOUQUETTE

JEFF REARDON   RICH GEDMAN

LOU MERLONI   TONY CONIGLIARO

JOE MORGAN

JERRY REMY

"With all due respect to **Ted Williams**, **Conigliaro** should at his present progress exceed the great record that Williams established. Not in batting average, but in **home runs** and **runs batted in** and certainly in **defensive play**."

— FROM AN AMERICAN LEAGUE TEAM'S SCOUTING REPORT

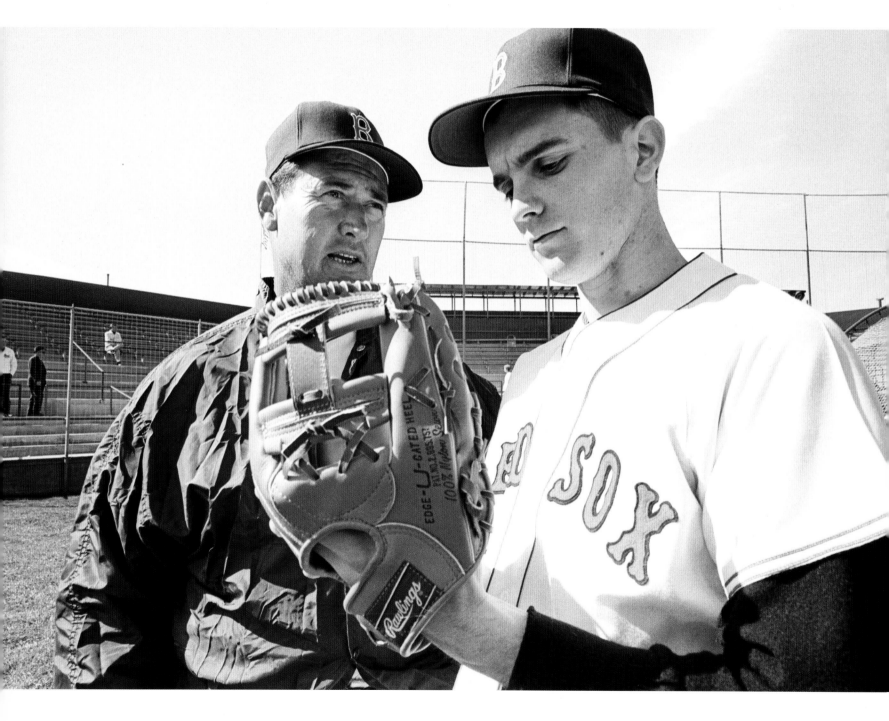

Conigliaro batted .290 and hit 24 home runs in 1964 at the age of 19. He would have hit more homers but for the six weeks he missed late in the season after a pitch broke his right arm. The following season, he slammed 32 homers, becoming the youngest AL player ever to win a home run title. "Some say he was the best-looking young hitter they've ever seen," said Pesky. Remembers Jim Kaat, then a young pitcher for the Minnesota Twins, "Tony C had the perfect swing for Fenway Park: Great power, lots of lift. He would have hit a lot of home runs there." The most similar ballplayers at age 20 in baseball history were Mickey Mantle and Frank Robinson, both Hall of Famers. One team's scouting report read, "With all due respect to Ted Williams, Conigliaro should at his present progress exceed the great record that Williams established. Not in batting average, but in home runs and runs batted in and certainly in defensive play."

Conigliaro played just as hard off the field. He was single, good-looking, had gaggles of girls following him, and enjoyed every minute of it. Teeny-boppers would drive to the family's home at 35 Parsons Drive and ask to see Tony; he would look out the window to see how attractive they were before deciding if he was home. He jumped on stage in nightclubs to sing, and even recorded a few singles, "Little Red Scooter" and "Playing the Field." He tantalized girls by declaring his permanent bachelorhood. Mod before anyone really knew what mod was, Tony C loved to flaunt his wares. Infielder Dick Williams was assigned to room with him on road trips in 1964 to lend a veteran influence. "The setup lasted just two months," Williams later said. "Because during that time, I never saw him. Not late at night, not first thing in the morning, never. I was providing veteran influence to a suitcase."

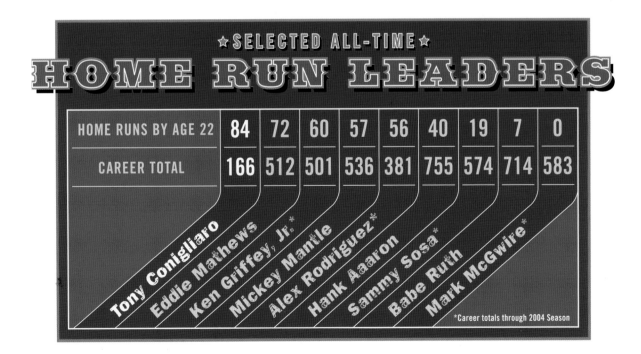

★SELECTED ALL-TIME★
HOME RUN LEADERS

	Tony Conigliaro	Eddie Mathews	Ken Griffey, Jr.*	Mickey Mantle	Alex Rodriguez*	Hank Aaaron	Sammy Sosa*	Babe Ruth	Mark McGwire*
HOME RUNS BY AGE 22	84	72	60	57	56	40	19	7	0
CAREER TOTAL	166	512	501	536	381	755	574	714	583

*Career totals through 2004 Season

There was no greater sign of Conigliaro's cockiness than the way he crowded the plate. Leaning in with his bat at the ready, almost daring pitchers to throw him inside, he often would not even jump out of the way when a pitch came sailing at him — he would move only his arm, his leg, his head, to get out of the way. That is the way of a legend. Says former teammate Ken Harrelson, "Once Tony got in the box, he was there. If you threw at his ribs, that's where you hit him. If you threw at his hands, that's where you hit him. If you threw at his knee, that's where you hit him. He just did not move. He was totally fearless." Chicago White Sox manager Al Lopez is quoted in *Tony C* as saying, "He attacks the ball. Those are the guys who are great hitters. But I must say this: If he continues to stand as close to the plate as he does and his reflexes and reactions don't become much sharper, he's going to get hit often and will be in danger of getting seriously injured. The pitchers simply aren't going to let him keep on challenging them the way he does right now. They'll throw in on him." Red Sox coach Bobby Doerr would pitch tennis balls inside to Conigliaro so the kid could practice getting out of the way. But Tony C paid little mind. He told the Record-American in January 1966, "I'm not going to change my batting style. You just can't let the pitchers force you into that in the major leagues or you're a dead duck."

Red Sox fans know where they were when Jack Hamilton's fastball cracked into Tony Conigliaro's face like a lightning bolt. It shares the where-were-you-when-JFK-was-shot horror, resonating with the same sudden senselessness. The newspaper pictures of Tony C in the hospital, his left eye so grotesquely swollen shut and black that it looked as if it had been torn from his skull, hit fans with such force they felt like they too had been hit by Hamilton.

MANAGER OF THE BOSTON RED SOX

1988-1991

JOE MORGAN

Walpole, Massachusetts

CAREER STATS

G	W	L	PCT
563	301	262	.535

Former Red Sox manager Joe Morgan grew up in Walpole, Massachusetts, and has lived there all his life. He spent 40 years in professional baseball, including managing the Red Sox from the middle of the 1988 season through 1991.

"I remember we would get on a bus in Walpole Center and it would drop us off on Huntington Avenue by Wentworth Institute. Then we would walk across the Fens to the park. *The thing I will always remember is one minute you were in the middle of the city with concrete, and cars and buses, and the next minute you would come out of the tunnel and there was this beautiful ballpark.*

"We used to go to as many doubleheaders as we could; two for the price of one. We tried to get there early so we could watch batting practice. When I first watched the Red Sox they had players like Lefty Grove and Joe Cronin. My favorite was Jimmie Foxx. I used to love watching his long home runs.

"My first and only at bat in Fenway Park came in 1959 when I was playing for the Kansas City Athletics. I hit a triple off the left-center field wall. Not many guys can say they have a lifetime average of 1.000 in Fenway Park.

"I was named interim manager of the Red Sox on July 14, 1988. My first time out on the field as manager was to check on the rain. The game was called at 9:30 p.m. that night. The team went on to win 12 straight games, so I was undefeated as manager for 13 days."

1969-1980

CARLTON FISK

Charlestown, New Hampshire

CAREER STATS

G	AB	R	H	HR	RBI	AVG
2499	8756	1276	2356	376	1130	.269

Former Red Sox catcher Carlton Fisk, a member of the Baseball Hall of Fame, was born in Bellows Falls, Vermont, and grew up in Charlestown, New Hampshire.

"I was a big Red Sox fan growing up. When I first started following the team, Ted Williams was in his final years. Then I got to watch Carl Yastrzemski in his early years. It was a big thrill to play with Yaz later on.

"It was a long trip from Charlestown to Fenway Park. I'm not sure how old I was when I went to my first game, but I remember they played the Detroit Tigers.

"I can remember looking down at the field and thinking how great it would be to play there."

"What I remember best about my first game at Fenway was walking into the dugout and looking out at the left-field wall. I couldn't believe how big it was and how green it was.

"After I went to Chicago, I used to look in a mirror and see myself in a White Sox uniform and wonder what I was doing there. There was never any doubt that I would go into the Hall of Fame with a Red Sox cap. I grew up a Red Sox fan. I played for the team — not many New Hampshire boys get to do that."

The 1967 season — "The Impossible Dream" season — had been marching on with a quickening drumbeat. The American League could not wipe its feet on the Red Sox anymore. Boston, Minnesota, Detroit and Chicago were fighting for the pennant in the most entangled four-team race the major leagues had ever seen. The tension went far beyond that for the Red Sox. Dick Williams had returned as a militaristic manager, clashing openly with youngsters George Scott, Mike Ryan, Rico Petrocelli and, most of all, Conigliaro. The charismatic Tony C's style differed with Yastrzemski's all business approach. But they were yin and yang batting third and fourth. Yaz was on his way to a Triple Crown. Conigliaro made two superb catches in the All-Star Game (the first ever televised in prime time) and on July 23 the 22-year-old slugger hit the 100th home run of his career — the youngest American League player ever to reach that level.

Then came the moment that will forever sadden Red Sox fans. Batting against the Angels' Hamilton on August 18, a pitch sailed in on him with such unforgiving swiftness that Conigliaro barely could flinch in defense. He undoubtedly thought the ball would defer to him, bent by youth's magnetic field. It did not. "As soon as it crunched into me," he said later, "it felt as if the ball would go in my head and come out the other side." The pitch cracked Conigliaro's cheekbone, dislocated his jaw, severely bruised his left eye, and caused such damage inside his mouth that it filled with liquid and left him gasping for air, wondering if he would suffocate right there in the Fenway Park dirt.

"Had the pitch been two inches higher," the team physician said the next day, "Tony would have been dead." Responding to the 10,000 pieces of fan mail that flooded Sancta Maria Hospital, Conigliaro boldly declared he probably would be back in a few weeks.

Of course, he wasn't. Beyond the blurriness, a cyst on Conigliaro's retina caused a blind spot at the focal point of his already limited vision. He didn't play as the Red Sox still captured the AL pennant and played the Cardinals in the World Series, losing in seven games. It is painfully poignant for Boston fans to remember that Conigliaro's replacements, Ken Harrelson and Jose Tartabull, batted .115 combined in the World Series.

Conigliaro reported to spring training the following year, but it soon was evident that he was half-blind — he hit .125 with no home runs in the exhibition season. His frustration boiling, he tore up the clubhouse, throwing stools and flinging uniforms, as the realization of a career's transience overtook him. Conigliaro's vision was 20-300 and he risked permanent blindness if he continued to play. On April 4, 1968, the same day Martin Luther King Jr. was assassinated, Tony C retired. (Conigliaro sat out the 1968 season before returning in 1969.) Fans wrote and offered to donate one of their eyes. Their hero looked fine from the outside, still the strong, handsome young man he had been a year earlier. But from inside, his life had become a blur. So desperate to play again, Conigliaro considered becoming a left-handed batter; he even tried to become a pitcher in the 1968 fall instructional league.

★ TONY C ★
A TIMELINE

1964	[04.64] Tony Conigliaro, a Revere native, is signed by the Boston Red Sox at the age of 19.
1965	
1966	[08.18.67] Tony is beaned by Angels pitcher Jack Hamilton. Hit in the left cheekbone, Conigliaro will miss the rest of 1967 and all of 1968. He was hitting .287 with 20 home runs and 67 RBIs in 95 games.
1967	
1968	
1969	[04.08.69] After a long recovery, Tony starts his first game for Boston. His dramatic two-run 10th-inning home run gives the Red Sox a brief lead, and his 12th-inning run wins it.
1970	
1971	[09.19.70] In a game against the Washington Senators, Tony and his brother Billy hit home runs for the Red Sox.
1972	
1973	
1974	[10.11.70] Tony is traded to the California Angels as part of a six-player swap.
1975	
1976	[07.12.71] Tony calls a 5 a.m. press conference to announce his retirement. Later tests will show that the sight in his left eye, injured in the 1967 beaning, had deteriorated.
1977	
1978	
1979	[03.05.75] Tony signs a contract with Pawtucket of the International League in an attempt to make a comeback.
1980	
1981	
1982	[01.09.82] Tony suffers a massive heart attack while being driven to the Boston airport by his brother Billy and lapses into a coma.
1983	
1984	
1985	[05.09.82] Tony emerges from the coma, but brain damage keeps him in a horrific state of virtual catatonia for the next eight years.
1986	
1987	
1988	[02.24.90] Tony dies of pneumonia and kidney failure at the age of 45.
1989	
1990	

MEMBER OF THE BOSTON RED SOX
1964 · 1970 · 1975

TONY CONIGLIARO
Revere, Massachusetts

CAREER STATS

G	AB	R	H	HR	RBI	AVG
876	3221	464	849	166	516	.264

JERRY REMY

Somerset, Massachusetts

CAREER STATS

G	AB	R	H	HR	RBI	AVG
1154	4455	605	1226	7	329	.275

Former Red Sox second baseman Jerry Remy grew up in Somerset, Massachusetts, a small town about 50 miles south of Boston. He became a Red Sox broadcaster in 1988.

"My grandfather and father took me to a lot of games at Fenway as a kid. I remember the long ride in on the Southeast Expressway and knowing that when I saw the light towers we were almost there. In those days not every game was televised and it was a big thrill to see a game.

The thing that impressed me most was coming up the runway into the park and seeing the field for the first time. I couldn't believe how green the field was and how high the left-field wall was. My favorite player was Yaz. If you were a young fan in 1967, he was the man. It was a tremendous thrill to become his teammate years later.

"I played very well at Fenway against the Red Sox, but it was really nerve wracking. It was the only time my family and friends got to see me play, so I was nervous, almost sick. After I was traded to the Red Sox, I became much more comfortable at Fenway. My family and friends got to see me on a regular basis so it took a lot of the pressure off. It's hard to believe, but I've now spent more time at Fenway as the TV color man than I did as a player."

By the next spring training, the clouds had begun to part. Conigliaro's vision had returned to virtually 20-20. Not quite the freakish 20-10 it had been, but good enough for him to start hitting home runs again. "Get the hell out of here!" he yelled at his first longball's persistent arc. Tony C seemed good as new — "I never saw the ball any better," he claimed — and he didn't take long to prove it. On Opening Day 1969 at Baltimore, he hit a 10th-inning home run and scored the winning run in the 12th as the Sox beat the Orioles, 5-4. "CONIGLIARO DOES IT!" the Record-American's front page screamed. A week later, in his first game back at Fenway Park, the crowd didn't wait for Conigliaro's name to be announced during pregame introductions. As soon as Sherm Feller uttered, "And No. 25…" the crowd let loose with what one newspaper called, "one of the greatest ovations ever tendered an athlete." During the ninth inning, a half-dozen jubilant fans hopped over the fence to mob Conigliaro in right field and congratulate him on his comeback. "Somebody Up There Likes Tony Conigliaro," read a Record-American headline.

Tony C batted .255 with 20 home runs and 82 RBIs in 1969, perhaps the most deserving player ever to be honored with the Comeback Player of the Year award. But he was having a harder time than anyone knew. Conigliaro couldn't pick up the spin on the baseball as well as he once did, and bright sunlight (at a time when many games were during the day) caused him severe headaches. At one point he complained about the glare off fans in Fenway Park's center field bleachers; the Red Sox responded by calling that section "Conig's Corner" and implored fans to wear dark-colored clothing to help their hero. With new layers added to his story, Conigliaro's celebrity grew: He enjoyed a salacious fling with Mamie Van Doren (who had appeared in Playboy) and made guest appearances on "To Tell The Truth," "The American Sportsman" and, naturally enough, "The Dating Game." He made such an impression on screen that a Hollywood movie producer, thinking a young unknown could be just what his film needed, considered Conigliaro to fill a role for a young Italian. Instead the producer chose Al Pacino. That movie was "The Godfather."

Conigliaro enjoyed perhaps his finest season in 1970 — 36 home runs and 116 RBIs — but behind his veil of normalcy his vision was getting progressively worse. He also was entangled in a not-particularly-private feud with teammates Carl Yastrzemski and Reggie Smith. After the season, the Red Sox did the unspeakable: They traded Tony C to the California Angels. He reported resentfully to his new team for the 1971 season, his decline accelerating. Conigliaro had been wrested from his Boston hometown and from his brother Billy, who had joined him in the Red Sox outfield. His nagging injuries while with the Angels branded him as a loafer (a curious reputation for someone with his proven ability to play through pain) and he had few friends on the club. He was playing horribly, batting .222 with four home runs on July 11, when he quite literally snapped.

During a 20-inning loss to the Oakland Athletics, in which he went 0-for-8 and struck out five times, Conigliaro got into two screaming matches with umpire George Anthony, charged after Anthony with his arms flailing wildly, and tossed his helmet in the air and hit it with his bat 50 feet down the first-base line. "The man belongs in an institution," Angels manager Lefty Phillips said, dead serious. Conigliaro pretty much agreed. He called a 5 a.m. press conference to announce his retirement. "I almost lost my mind out there in the field tonight. When I came back to the room, I was twitching and my stomach was in knots. I thought, 'What am I doing here?... It's something that had to be done or I'd be in a straitjacket with the rest of the nuts. I was on the ledge tonight." Then he revealed that his vision never had recovered from the 1967 beaning. The middle of his vision was 20-300. He had to look slightly away from the baseball to get any kind of look at it. "It's like a hole that will always be missing dead center in the eye. Whenever I focus on anything, there's a total blind spot. My eyesight never came back to normal. When the pitcher holds the ball, I can't see his hand or the ball. I pick up the spin on the ball late by looking away, to the side. I don't know how I do it. I kept it away from the Red Sox... I had a lot of headaches because of the strain to see, my search for that damn baseball."

1980-1990

RICH GEDMAN

Worcester, Massachusetts

CAREER STATS

G	AB	R	H	HR	RBI	AVG
1033	3159	331	195	88	382	.252

Former Red Sox catcher Rich Gedman grew up in Worcester, Massachusetts. *"My earliest memory of being a Red Sox fan is going to bed with a transistor radio to listen to Ned Martin broadcasting the games.* I was supposed to be asleep, but I would have the volume down real low. My parents never let on, but I think they knew what I was doing.

"I got to Fenway Park for the first time when I was 10 years old. My fifth grade teacher, Mr. Monfredo, knew how much I loved the Red Sox, and he was nice enough to take me. We sat right in the middle of the bleachers, where we had a good view of my favorite player, Carl Yastrzemski, in left field. I remember looking down at the field and thinking how great it would be to play for the team.

"When I got my Red Sox uniform on for the first time, I went out on the field to look around Fenway. Some fan kept hollering at me, 'Hey Dave!' Then I realized my uniform had been assigned to someone else during spring training. It was kind of humbling, but it brought me back to reality.

"I got in a little trouble with the fans when the papers quoted me as saying, 'Red Sox fans are fickle.' The fans thought I was criticizing them, but I really meant we are fickle. I still thought of myself as the kid up in the center-field bleachers."

Finally some sympathy was sent Tony C's way. Wrote Jim Murray in the Los Angeles Times, "If he took the batter's box with one leg, or one arm, or even one ear, the world would have been awed. But, to take the batter's box with one eye should be a more impressive show of courage.... Tony C could fool the eye doctors and the eye charts. He couldn't fool the pitchers or the curves. The good ones had no trouble with a one-eyed man."

received a three-minute ovation. Yet his age overtook his desire. He soon had hamstring and groin injuries that kept him out of the lineup, and he lost his role to Rice, who began to blossom. Batting just .123, Conigliaro was demoted to Class AAA Pawtucket in June. He hung 'em up in August. "My only regret is that I didn't get to play as a mature athlete," he later said. "If I stayed healthy, I would have given Aaron a shot."

"As soon as it crunched into me, it felt as if the ball would go in my head and come out the other side."

TONY C

And with that, Tony C was gone. He packed up, moved back to New England and opened a golf course and restaurant in Nahant a few miles south of Swampscott. In 1975 he got the itch to play again and at the age of 30, despite having not played competitively in almost four years, beat out Jim Rice (who had won the International League Triple Crown the previous season) as the Red Sox's designated hitter. Yet another amazing Tony C comeback was capped on Opening Day, April 8, when he singled at Fenway Park in the first inning and

Conigliaro became a successful television broadcaster in San Francisco — despite a Boston accent that overwhelmed even the strictest speech classes — thanks to his charm and affability. Critics claimed he was too clunky to even correctly pronounce his own name. "Yeah, but it's a tough name," he replied. In January 1982 he auditioned as the color man for Red Sox television broadcasts and was convinced he had the job. The next day his brother Billy was driving him to the airport for a flight to San Francisco where he planned to

MEMBER OF THE BOSTON RED SOX

1964-1967

MIKE RYAN

Haverhill, Massachusetts

CAREER STATS						
G	AB	R	H	HR	RBI	AVG
636	1920	146	370	28	161	.193

BOX SCORE
August 18, 1967

RED SOX 3, ANGELS 2

California	ab	r	h	rbi		Boston	ab	r	h	rbi
Cardenal cf	4	0	0	0		Andrews 2b	3	0	0	0
Fregosi ss	4	0	0	0		Adair 3b	3	0	1	0
Hall rf	4	2	2	2		Yastrzemski lf	3	0	0	0
Mincher 1b	4	0	1	0		Scott 1b	4	0	1	0
Reichardt lf	3	0	0	0		Smith cf	4	0	0	0
Rodgers c	2	0	0	0		Conigliaro rf	1	0	1	0
Knoop 2b	3	0	1	0		Tartabull rf	1	1	0	0
Werhas 3b	2	0	0	0		Petrocelli ss	3	2	1	1
Repoz ph	1	0	0	0		Howard c	3	0	0	0
Held 3b	0	0	0	0		Bell p	3	0	2	1
Hamilton p	1	0	0	0						
Satriano ph	1	0	0	0						
Kelso p	0	0	0	0						
Coates p	0	0	0	0						
Morton ph	1	0	0	0						
Cimino p	0	0	0	0						
Totals	30	2	4	2		Totals	28	3	6	2

California	ip	h	r	er	bb	k		Boston	ip	h	r	er	bb	k
Hamilton, LP	5	4	2	2	1	5		Bell, WP	9	4	2	2	1	5
Kelso	.2	1	1	1	2	0								
Coates	1.1	1	0	0	0	1								
Cimino	1	0	0	0	0	2								

California	000	000	101 – 2
Boston	000	201	00x – 3

E–Fregosi. DP–California, Boston. LOB–California 2, Boston 7. 2B–Bell.
3B–Petrocelli. HR–Hall 2(19). HBP–Conigliaro (by Hamilton)
T–2:16. A–31,207

Former Red Sox catcher Mike Ryan grew up in Haverhill, Massachusetts, just south of the New Hampshire border. His professional baseball career spanned 35 years; he was a member of the Red Sox's 1967 "Impossible Dream" team.

"As far back as I can remember, baseball was a major topic of conversation in our house. Whenever there was a family gathering, after we got caught up on the news, the conversation would turn to baseball.

"Jack Ryan, who was a cousin of my grandfather, caught for the Boston Beaneaters (later renamed the Braves) and played in the major leagues for 13 seasons. Jack was a coach for the Red Sox from 1923 to 1927. My Uncle Paul was a minor league pitcher, and my father was an outstanding athlete.

"I used to go to Fenway Park on the bus with the other kids from the local playground. We all fantasized about standing at home plate in a Red Sox uniform. We all dreamed about growing up to play for the Sox.

"The first time I played at Fenway Park I was 17 years old playing in a Hearst Corporation All-Star game. When I got to the big leagues with the Red Sox it was always a thrill to walk onto the field at Fenway. *I think every kid in New England dreams about playing for the Red Sox someday. I was fortunate enough that my dream came true.*"

MEMBER OF THE BOSTON RED SOX

'90-19

JEFF REARDON

Dalton, Massachusetts

CAREER STATS

W	L	PCT	G	SV	IP	SO	ERA
73	77	.487	880	367	1132	877	3.16

Former Red Sox reliever Jeff Reardon grew up in Dalton, Massachusetts, in the western part of the state, and graduated from the University of Massachusetts. He was a premier closer for 14 years in the major leagues, including three with the Red Sox.

"I was a big Red Sox fan from the time I was a little kid. I used to listen to Ned Martin broadcasting the games all the time. And I used to keep score while I listened to the games.

"I remember my first trip to Fenway Park was with one of the local youth groups. Before we went to the game we all had to go to church. We trouped into a church near Fenway, and there was Carl Yastrzemski sitting a couple of rows in front of us. The counselors kept telling us we couldn't bother him but we were pretty excited.

"My favorite Red Sox player was Jim Lonborg. I was a big Red Sox fan, but I always loved to watch Tom Seaver pitching for the Mets.

"When I joined the Red Sox I had been a big leaguer for 11 years, but it was still a big thrill to play in Fenway Park. *It was pretty ironic that I always sat way out in right field or the bleachers as a kid, and then I spent my whole career with the Red Sox out in the bullpen.* It was pretty easy to look around and spot where I used to sit."

wrap up his affairs when something went terribly wrong. Tony C stopped breathing, and he clutched his chest with his fists clenched. "A tear came out of his left eye," Billy said. Billy raced 85 mph down 1-A — the same speed and the same route Tony C used to drive to play at Fenway Park — to a hospital. The heart attack cost Tony C's brain six minutes of oxygen and left him in a deep coma. This otherwise healthy man, who never smoked, barely drank and exercised regularly, was only 37. The lightning of randomness had struck him again.

He emerged from the coma four months later, but brain damage kept Conigliaro in a state of virtual catatonia for the next eight years. Drooped in bed, barely able to move or speak, he left his family and friends to wonder if he had any idea what had happened to him. They were torn between hoping he didn't and hoping he did, because if the Tony C they knew remained in that body another comeback was just a matter of time. Recalls Billy, "I just kept looking at him: 'C'mon,

Tony, one more time. You have to come around.' It was torture for us for eight years — for him not being able to come out of it, when all the other times he had." Stickers sprouted on car bumpers all over Boston — I PRAY FOR TONY C — and a benefit starring Frank Sinatra helped pay for his mounting medical bills. The torture crawled on, year by excruciating year. By the time Conigliaro died of pneumonia and kidney failure on February 24, 1990, it rang less of misfortune than mercy.

The legacy he left is far more complex than that of fellow teen idol James Dean or even New England's Kennedys. It goes beyond the fact that Tony C might have become one of the greatest home run hitters baseball has ever known. Former Red Sox manager Billy Herman once described Tony C's home runs as "the kind Ruth and Gehrig and Foxx used to hit." But Tony C's was an arc interrupted; he lives on as much a symbol of reverberative youth and promise as

Red Sox utility player Lou Merloni grew up in Framingham, Massachusetts, less than an hour's drive from Fenway Park. "I was about seven years old when I came to my first game. My father took me to a lot of games, and we came to the Yankees games any time we could. I got to see how the fans felt about those games. As soon as we got here, I wanted to run up the walkway to get a look at the field and see the Green Monster.

"My favorite player was Wade Boggs. I used to watch him very closely, and I was amazed at the things he could do with a bat. When his number (26) became available when I was rookie, I grabbed it. It's a big thrill to be wearing my hero's uniform number.

"My first game at Fenway happened to be the day of my parents' 33rd wedding anniversary. I had a limo pick them up to take them to the game. I had always told them that when I made it to the major leagues I would have a limousine take them to the park. My sister drove me to the game so I could ride home with my parents. She was more nervous than I was. I told her, *'All I want to do is hit a double off the wall, slide safely into second, then dust my self off, and take a minute to look around.'* My first time up, I hit a home run. About the time I was rounding second base the fans picked up the chant, 'Lou! Lou! Lou!' It's something I'll never forget."

MEMBER OF THE BOSTON RED SOX
'98-20

LOU MERLONI
Framingham, Massachusetts

CAREER STATS						
G	AB	R	H	HR	RBI	AVG
409	1061	136	290	14	123	.273

* Through 2004 season

---

of Sisyphian persistence, of finally succumbing to one too many tragedies. His mother, Teresa, lamented, "Every time he was happiest, he got knocked down. He got beaned in Boston when he was doing so great. When he was excited he got knocked down." A Boston radio show in January 2001 paid tribute to Conigliaro; the host told the audience, "I listened to about six hours of tape the other day. I was crying, thinking of how alive he was, how vibrant he was, how much he loved playing baseball, how much he loved playing for the Red Sox." And Red Sox fans loved him for it. Still do.

"There isn't one day goes by where I don't hear something about him from somebody," says Tony C's youngest brother, Richie. "I had my finger fixed the other day. This Dr. Yee, he says, 'Conigliaro? You're not related to Tony, are ya? Oh, he was my favorite player,' this and that. Every time, everywhere I go when I say the name, it still means something. This nun from New York: 'Tony Conigliaro! I loved Tony C!' Another time, I was in Las Vegas. I give the guy at the crap table my card. 'Conigliaro? That's not Tony, is it?' Everywhere I go. It's been so long. But people don't forget."

They don't forget the fighter who came back not once, but twice, after sitting out more than a season. They don't forget the image of his maimed eye. They don't forget him hamming it up on the "Merv Griffin Show," living life with flair and fullness and dating every pretty girl. They don't forget the home runs he launched over the Green Monster. And most of all, they don't forget that Tony Conigliaro once was just like them, growing up in East Boston, dreaming of playing ball forever. The kid practiced his stroke by swinging at a lit candle, becoming so precise he could put out the flame as the barrel whooshed by. The candle never fell over.

It still hasn't. And the way New England remembers Tony C, it probably never will.

The All-Time Starting Nine

THE GENIUS OF PEDRO MARTINEZ

Martinez showed the Red Sox faithful
a rare arm and heart, in addition
to a great mind for pitching.

THE GENIUS OF PEDRO MARTINEZ

Press the rewind button. To find the real Pedro Martinez, you have to reverse the tape, go back in time. Fastballs zip from the catcher back to his fingers. The changeups float back. All those zeroes vanish from the scoreboards, the flag-waving crowds return home, he gets traded from the Red Sox back to the Expos and then to the Dodgers. The brawls untangle, he returns to the minors, to Triple-A, to Double-A, to Class A and beyond, all the way back to 1990 and inside the Great Falls, Montana, Dodgers team bus, traveling down one of the Pioneer League's lonely highways.

"What you got for me today?" the 150-pound pitcher said, jumping into a seat next to Guy Conti, the Great Falls Dodgers pitching coach. They had a deal: a word a day. Other players listened to stereos and played cards; most just sleep. But the hyperactive pitcher, Pedro Martinez from Manoguayabo, Dominican Republic, wanted to l earn a new word.

Didn't matter what word — shoe, tractor, medicine. Conti gave Martinez the word and had him spell it, then use it in a sentence. They read signs posted on the highway and discussed what they meant. Over and over they did this as the bus rambled through Montana, Idaho, Utah. When Conti slept, Pedro read newspapers, Sports Illustrated, anything. "He was clamoring to learn," Conti says. "You couldn't give him enough."

Most of the players who came to the United States from the Los Angeles Dodgers' academy in the Dominican Republic would shy away from learning English, intimidated by the unfamiliar. But not this kid. Unleashed upon a world he found fascinating, not frightening, he wanted to soak it all up in a hurry. Move up. Be like Ramon, his big brother and idol, who was becoming a 20-game winner with the Dodgers. Be the best.

Those days were all about learning. English or baseball — give it to Pedro, and give it to him now. He learned about mechanics. He learned about the changeup. He learned the words, then the phrases, then the idioms of English, all of it feeding his growing confidence. When the Helena Brewers manager threatened him with a beanball war, the kid looked him straight in the eye and said, "That's OK. Just remember: Your kid's throwing 84; I'm throwing 94."

That kind of velocity is hardly uncommon in baseball, but what sets apart Martinez is that his mind is just as quick. He shot up the Dodgers' minor league ladder in 1991, advancing from Class A to Double-A to Triple-A, gobbling up his lessons with striking ease and hunger. He was different. That 5-foot-10 kid, now up to 170 pounds, had a mind like a sponge and eyes like lasers.

This background information helps explain why nine years after those Great Falls bus rides, then-Red Sox manager Jimy Williams sat in his office after another sterling Pedro Martinez performance just shaking his head. All Williams could say was: "Do you realize what you're watching?" Whatever it was, we had never seen anything quite like it. Baseball has had its share of modern power-pitching legends, Nolan Ryan and Roger Clemens,

Dwight Gooden and Randy Johnson shooting across its sky — but never one quite like Martinez, whose dominance derives as much from his brain as his body. Entering the 2005 season, Martinez was the leader among active pitchers in career ERA (2.71), opponents batting average (.209) and getting taped to a dugout pole by teammates (one). Yet he has the physical stature of a real pitcher left in the dryer too long. The naïve would mistake him for a mascot, a good-luck charm to be worn around the neck.

When Martinez stands atop the mound, baseball in hand, he doesn't just say, "You have no chance," which would suffice. He says, "I know more than you." And he proceeds to prove it. Perhaps his most defining moment came when he

joined in the salute as race and class lines crossed like the tangled Beantown streets outside. Boston embraced Pedro Martinez as fondly and possessively as it did its domestic Hall of Famers, like Ted Williams, or exotic characters, like Luis Tiant. El Tiante was known for smoking cigars. Pedro? Smoking hitters.

Martinez joined the Red Sox in 1998, and for seven seasons he won an astounding 76 percent of the time. His record over that period was 117-37, with a 2.52 ERA and two Cy Young awards. Martinez's final appearance for the Red Sox came in Game Three of the 2004 World Series. He pitched seven scoreless innings against the St. Louis Cardinals, and a day later the Red Sox won their first world championship in 86 years. New England's joy was at a roar for weeks, tempered only

When Martinez studies opposing hitters, he scans for the emotional as much as the physical. "I look for everything — attitudes, frustrations, weakness," he says. "I look for everything I can look for to learn and that's gonna help my game. Sometimes you can see that with just one pitch you can frustrate the whole game — with one batter. There's some of them that will let one at-bat frustrate them forever. All you have to do is get a pitch that's one inch away from the plate from some hitters and that will get them dragging all day and get them upset. It takes away their whole game."

entered Game Five of the 1999 American League Division Series against the Cleveland Indians with the score 8-8 in the fourth inning. Martinez had not started the game and was in pain because of a pulled muscle behind his shoulder blade. But he spooked the Indians to the point where he gave up no hits in six scoreless innings, winning the game, 12-8, and the series for Boston. It was his signature performance, the one that someday could be engraved on his Hall of Fame plaque. "He brought normalcy to the game," then-Red Sox pitching coach Joe Kerrigan said afterward. "That's Pedro. That's the legend of Pedro."

That legend grew with every game that Martinez pitched for the Red Sox, particularly at Fenway Park. Dominican fans waved flags of their home country, and their chants of "Pe-dro! Pe-dro!" echoed throughout the secular cathedral. Traditional Red Sox fans

when Martinez decided to leave Boston and accept a richer contract offer from the New York Mets.

Martinez developed an eerie, Buddha-like presence in baseball, a cherubic runt equal parts pitcher and poet. When Paul O'Neill played for the New York Yankees, he rarely referred to Martinez by name, instead calling him "that little Dominican fellow" — out of an abundance of respect, not a lack of it. Martinez commanded the same from the press, using his precise and measured English to both inform and scold, tickle and intimidate.

The Red Sox's all-time team is a who's-who of baseball history, with names like Williams, Foxx, Yastrzemski and more. Few modern players are deemed worthy of being compared with such hallowed greats. Yet Martinez not only is the best of his era; he would have dominated against anyone. His road to Boston was

Martinez pitching at Fenway Park was a special occasion. Dominican Republic fans waved flags of their home country, and their chants of "Pe-dro! Pe-dro!" echoed throughout the secular cathedral. Traditional Red Sox fans joined in the salute as race and class lines crossed like the tangled Beantown streets outside.

as unique and stark as his repertoire. That little Dominican fellow wasn't merely inside the bus anymore — he was driving it. "Once every five days," Red Sox catcher Jason Varitek once said, "New England becomes Pedro's world. The rest of us just work here."

When Martinez studies opposing hitters, he scans for the emotional as much as the physical. "I look for everything — attitudes, frustrations, weakness," he says. "Some of them will let one at-bat frustrate them forever. All you have to do is get a pitch that's one inch away from the plate from some hitters and that will get them dragging all day and get them upset. It takes away their whole game. Sometimes I look in a batter's face for almost a minute before I pitch, just to see his attitude, his eyes, what they're gonna say."

EVEN BASEBALL'S TOP SLUGGERS ARE AT A LOSS WHEN ASKED HOW TO HIT AGAINST MARTINEZ. "FOR ONE, YOU GO TO CHURCH IN THE MORNING," ALEX RODRIGUEZ SAYS. "HE ALWAYS KNOWS WHAT THE HITTER'S THINKING. IF HE THREW 84, 85, HE COULD STILL GET EVERYBODY OUT. HE'S THAT SMART."

Like many pitchers, Martinez keeps a mental book on batters. But more than their tendencies and power zones, he senses when a hitter might be most likely to dive in to a pitch, when he isn't tracking the ball well, when he's bailing off the plate. Once an aspiring doctor — he still reads medical books from time to time — Martinez takes full X-rays of hitters when they step to the plate. Emotional MRIs.

Even baseball's top sluggers are at a loss when asked how to hit against Martinez. "For one, you go to church in the morning," Alex Rodriguez says. "He always knows what the hitter's thinking. If he threw 84, 85, he could still get everybody out. He's that smart." Before his magical 1999 postseason heroics against the Indians, Martinez sat down in the dugout next to Boston's starter that day, Bret Saberhagen, and said, "These guys are gonna swing

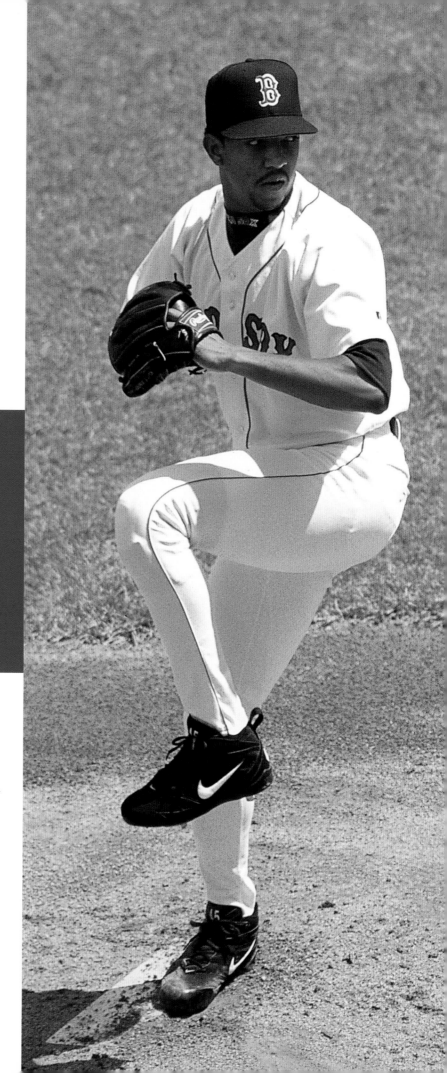

tonight. You don't have to throw them strikes." Saberhagen later acknowledged he failed to do that, got shelled, and needed Martinez to bail out the Red Sox, to show them the way.

When he was the Red Sox manager, Jimy Williams almost never removed Martinez in the middle of an inning. Williams trusted Pedro to extricate himself from whatever trouble he encountered, using memory to recall the past and intellect to foresee the future. This process is overshadowed when Martinez unleashes one of his five darting fastballs, a wicked curve or a changeup with more movement than a belly dancer. It's easier to see in Greg Maddux, for example, whose mortal repertoire brings his brain to the fore. But even Maddux appreciates Martinez' s control tower more than his rockets. "He's

Glavine, who became Martinez's teammate in 2005: "He's elevated himself to another category. That gives him a mystique about him. They're almost beat before the game even starts, they're so psyched out."

After Martinez dominated the Yankees 13-1 in Game Three of the 1999 American League Championship Series, the series effectively had been shortened to six games. All of baseball spoke of how the Yankees, their lead cut to two games to one, had better close out the Red Sox before a seventh game, when Martinez surely would smother them as he had everyone else — particularly the Indians in his Game Five relief gem in the previous round.

During that game with the Indians, Cleveland catcher Sandy Alomar tried a little gamesmanship by retying

"HE'S CAPABLE OF BLOWING A LOT OF HITTERS AWAY, BUT HE TRICKS THEM."
GREG MADDUX

capable of blowing a lot of hitters away, but he tricks them," Maddux says. "I like the embarrassment he puts on hitters, the way he abuses them and makes them look like they don't belong on the same field with him. There's a lot of pitchers with stuff as good as his. But he says, 'Even though I'm a power pitcher, I can still pitch like I'm not.' "

Hitters like to say that the game is 90 percent mental — until they are overmatched. Then the pitcher simply has "filthy" stuff. "The bottom line is he throws three pitches and can throw them at any time in the count," says Derek Jeter of the Yankees. There is something else at work, too — an aura that erodes a batter's confidence when Pedro stares at him. Says Mets pitcher Tom

his shoes after reaching first base in an attempt to slow down Martinez. The pitcher merely smirked at Alomar, as if to say, "Don't mess with the master." He delivered that message through his last pitch before being hoisted atop his teammates' shoulders.

Without his best stuff that night or in his next start against the Yankees, Martinez had to rely on spotting his pitches, on changing speeds. Pitching sequences and patterns. This is a man who, when he demonstrates three different grips of a changeup, moving fingers across and with the seams, looks like a pianist forming a chord. His art emerged those nights against the Indians and the Yankees, leaving Yankees manager Joe Torre to say, "He's got a baseball instead of a paintbrush."

Listening to Martinez speak rivals watching him pitch. To him, games aren't "big," they "have meaning." Dominicans are his "fellows." When then-Red Sox shortstop Nomar Garciaparra had a big game against the Indians a few years ago, teammate Trot Nixon gushed, "Nomar's awesome, he's just a flat-out stud." Martinez described Nomar as "rich in talent," a phrase Boston writers still speak of reverently.

Martinez makes eye contact during interviews — a welcome change from many major leaguers, most of whom adopt an airy gaze, as if playing dead before a bear — and will explain himself calmly, repeatedly, if not understood. Says Tony Massarotti, who covers the Red Sox for the Boston Herald, "You feel like you're talking to a diplomat."

On days that Martinez pitches though, his brain turns on, his eyes lock in, and nothing else exists. "A bomb could go off next to him and he wouldn't notice," says Kerrigan, his former pitching coach. Martinez recognizes when the spotlight is on him, and thrives on it. No onlooker will forget his 17-strikeout one-hitter at Yankee Stadium in September 1999, when he made the Yankees look like the Gas House Gorillas: One, two, three strikes, you're out…one, two, three strikes, you're out… The following season, he out-dueled former Red Sox ace Roger Clemens in beating the Yankees 2-0 on national television.

Martinez has shed the head-hunting label he gained in the mid-1990s while pitching for the Montreal Expos, when he had

Dissatisfied with knowing all the current baseball idioms, Martinez became the new Dennis Eckersley, coining his own vernacular." On days he was not pitching, the hyperactive Martinez passed time chirping these phrases from the dugout. In 1999, the chatter so vexed the Chicago White Sox that they called the Red Sox's dugout and told them to shut him up. Garciaparra and pitcher Mark Portugal proceeded to tape Martinez's mouth closed, and then for good measure tie him to a dugout support pole. This topped the previous best dugout stories about Martinez, which included him wearing a Yoda mask during a game and, another time, parading around in the uniform pants of puffy reliever Rich Garces, who could audition as the Michelin man.

little control of his pitches. But he doesn't mince words when discussing his art of intimidation, which has helped make the 5-foot-11, 175-pound wisp the biggest bully in the big leagues. "You don't intimidate the guy — the ball does," Martinez says. "A man is just a man. Not because you're 6-foot-7 and I'm 5-foot-11 are you gonna intimidate me. If I reach back and throw a ball at your head, 98 mph, there's a big chance that if the ball hits you in the head, you're gonna get something broken, and really bad. Sometimes, letting them know that you're crazy enough to do anything with that ball in your hands, it's good enough to give them an impression."

Indeed, the diplomat is not always diplomatic. When asked

about the Curse of the Bambino after shutting out the Yankees at Fenway Park in May 2001, Martinez snapped, "Maybe they should wake up the Bambino and have him face me and maybe I'll drill him." No doubt. When Matt Lawton stepped out of the batter's box just as Martinez was about to pitch to him in a 1999 game against the Minnesota Twins, Martinez hit Lawton in the right knee. After Olmado Saenz, batting for the Oakland Athletics, made no effort to get out of the way of a Martinez pitch, Martinez buried a fastball in Saenz's back, as if to say, "You want to get hit? Try this on for size."

"If you get fresh with me on the mound or do something to show me up," Martinez said after hitting Saenz, "I'll drill you."

important," says Ramon, who retired from baseball in 2001. "We all went to school. Sometimes we didn't want to, but we had to. It was very important. They were like, 'You can play, but you have to go to school.'"

The same deal remained after Pedro signed with the Dodgers as a 16-year-old and entered their baseball academy in Guerra, a 45-minute bus ride from home. He had to finish high school at night. But he spent every free moment playing baseball, coming home with his school uniform dusty from the sandlots. He reluctantly decided to break his mother's heart.

"I'm almost falling asleep on the bus. I'm trying to read the books," Pedro recalls. "So maybe I should concentrate on one. And

Paulino and Leopoldina Martinez always made sure their four sons — Ramon, Nelson, Pedro and Jesus — had the proper uniform for Liceo Secondario las Americas, the high school in Manoguayabo. Khaki pants and a blue shirt. Paulino worked as an administrator at the school. Leopoldina washed the uniforms every day to make sure they looked proper.

Pedro got his best grades in English. "Lowest grade I ever had was a 98," he crows. "I was straight aces." An aspiring physician, Pedro wanted to play baseball, too, particularly after big brother Ramon started succeeding with the Dodgers. His parents kept the hyper kid as focused as they could. "Education was very

I didn't want to quit baseball because baseball was No. 1. I decided baseball didn't go along with medicine. I told my mom and she started crying. I was too good in school to just quit it like that."

Pedro's brain didn't lie fallow at the Dodgers' academy. He soaked up all he could — particularly during the morning and evening English classes that were required of all players. Pablo Peguero, the scout who signed Martinez, remembers, "The only complaint we had from teachers was that Pedro talked too much. He asked a lot of questions. He wanted to learn fast." Adds Mel Didier, then a special-assignment scout with the Dodgers, "He was a guy, from the first day he was with the Dodgers, who picked up all the defenses, backups, cutoffs, relays. He did it in three weeks.

[PEDRO MARTINEZ]
LEADS ACTIVE PITCHERS IN THE
FOLLOWING CATEGORIES
[THROUGH 2004 SEASON]

WINNING PERCENTAGE
.705

QUALITY STARTS PERCENTAGE
.704

Ks/WALKS RATIO
4.17 TO 1

HITS PER 9 INNINGS
6.84

BASERUNNERS PER 9 INNINGS
9.26

OPPONENTS BATTING AVERAGE
.209

OPPONENTS ON-BASE AVERAGE
.271

OPPONENTS SLUGGING AVERAGE
.311

"SOMETIMES, LETTING THEM KNOW THAT YOU'RE CRAZY ENOUGH TO DO ANYTHING WITH THAT BALL IN YOUR HANDS, IT'S GOOD ENOUGH TO GIVE THEM AN IMPRESSION."

PEDRO ON THE ALL-TIME LISTS

Ks PER 9 INNINGS		OPPONENTS BATTING AVG		HITS PER 9 INNINGS		Ks/WALKS RATIO		WINNING PERCENTAGE	
Randy Johnson	11.12	Nolan Ryan	.204	Nolan Ryan	6.56	**Pedro Martinez**	**4.17 to 1**	Al Spalding	.795
Kerry Wood	10.43	Sandy Koufax	.205	Sandy Koufax	6.79	Curt Schilling	4.04 to 1	Spud Chandler	.717
Pedro Martinez	**10.40**	**Pedro Martinez**	**.209**	**Pedro Martinez**	**6.84**	Mike Mussina	3.42 to 1	**Pedro Martinez**	**.705**
Nolan Ryan	9.55	Andy Messersmith	.212	Sid Fernandez	6.85	Bret Saberhagen	3.40 to 1	Tim Hudson	.702
Sandy Koufax	9.28	Randy Johnson	.213	J.R. Richard	6.88	Brad Radke	3.18 to 1	Whitey Ford	690

[THROUGH 2004 SEASON]

PEDRO WITH FELIPE ALOU

Some guys spend three years and never do."

Martinez spent two years studying in Guerra before graduating to the United States in 1990, determined to move up quickly. Forbidden to run so that he could gain weight, he bribed a ballpark guard with $20 bills to let him run at night. Guy Conti, his bus-ride English teacher in Great Falls, once gave in and let Martinez run a two-mile race against 20 other pitchers; Martinez won, and afterward was seen puking out his guts.

In 1991, after little more than a year in the United States, Martinez had risen to Triple-A Albuquerque. During a road trip to Las Vegas, longtime baseball executive Syd Thrift, then a consultant to the Dodgers, was in his hotel room when Martinez knocked on the door. "I want to be the best," Martinez told Thrift, and the two talked for more than an hour about focus and concentration. Thrift filed the following report to then-general manager Fred Claire: "Great aptitude. Came to meet me voluntarily. Wanted to learn more about how to be successful. Could be a great one!"

The Dodgers used Martinez as a middle reliever in 1992 and 1993 before trading him to the Expos because they believed his body wouldn't withstand the rigors of pitching. Though broken-hearted to leave Ramon, Martinez found an equally important influence in Montreal: manager Felipe Alou, an erudite fellow Dominican known for his equanimity and poise. "You can't overestimate the influence that Felipe had on Pedro," says Kerrigan, the Expos' pitching coach from 1992 to 1996. "He was like his parish priest. He was like his father. Whenever Pedro strayed a little bit or drifted a little bit, Felipe would bring him back in. The long talks that they had during Pedro's

maturing years have paid off now. You're seeing the result of that." Adds Martinez, "I would say 70 percent of my career has to do with the mental approach that Felipe taught me. He taught me everything I know about approaching the game and taking it serious — especially on the day I was starting. Felipe always told me: On that day you are somebody special. That's your day."

Martinez made Montreal his city. He became a crowd favorite because he was so small, so feisty (he precipitated several brawls) and so dominant (he pitched nine perfect innings in 1995 before losing the gem in the 10th). Martinez returned the affection by learning French through television and the local newspapers, and by speaking with locals around town. During his Cy Young Award season of 1997, when he was honored at a downtown restaurant for being named National League pitcher of the month for July, he delivered his acceptance speech in French, and received a standing ovation.

Soon after Martinez joined the Red Sox the following year, ballparks around the American League began trembling with chants of "Pe-dro! Pe-dro!" Martinez's pitches and persona captivated anyone who watched; he was not a favorite just in Boston. His magnetism was unmatched. Alex Rodriguez made more news with his pocketbook than his performance. Mark McGwire and Sammy Sosa might have painted a forceful stroke or two in an eruption of muscular might. But only from Pedro could you get two hours of adrenaline, finesse and art on a regular basis.

He understood his stature, having earned it, and bristled at any suggestion to the contrary. Martinez caused a stir in 1999 by speaking out when Jimy Williams scratched him from a scheduled start because he arrived late to Fenway Park. "He didn't have any reason to embarrass me out there. If I'm a bad influence on the team, they'd better get me out of here," Martinez said. Yet his self-regard has strict limits. Any hint that he has eclipsed his big brother as a pitcher is met with a stern and stock reply. "A student," he warns, "can't ever be smarter than his teacher."

It was with this reverence that Martinez had one of the thrills of his life at the 1999 All-Star Game at Fenway Park — and it had nothing to do with him striking out the first five batters he faced as the American League's starting pitcher. Hours later, well past midnight, he went to the ballpark suite of Red Sox owner John Harrington and met Ted Williams. Martinez peppered Williams with questions about hitters, deliveries,

the effectiveness of curveballs versus changeups...for an hour and a half, leaving all who saw it with their mouths agape. Williams autographed a program for Martinez — and when the pitcher left the room, he clutched that program in his two hands, not the All-Star Game MVP trophy.

Martinez said thank you to all of his teachers — from his parents to Ramon to Conti to Thrift to Alou to Williams and more — when he spoke one morning to a Boston-area elementary school assembly. From the podium he looked out upon the sea of white tops with navy blue pants and skirts, flashed back to his youth, and smiled. "You look great in those uniforms," he told the kids. The best pitcher in the world nodded to the children's cheers, naked for everyone to see.

BASEBALL HAS HAD ITS SHARE OF MODERN POWER-PITCHING LEGENDS, NOLAN RYAN AND ROGER CLEMENS AND DWIGHT GOODEN AND RANDY JOHNSON SHOOTING ACROSS ITS SKY — BUT NEVER ONE QUITE LIKE MARTINEZ, WHOSE DOMINANCE DERIVES AS MUCH FROM HIS BRAIN AS HIS BODY.

ALL-TIME BATTING ORDER

by JOHNNY PESKY	by CHARLIE WAGNER
Dom DiMaggio (or Fred Lynn), CF	Dom DiMaggio, CF
Nomar Garciaparra, SS	Bobby Doerr, 2B
Ted Williams, LF	Ted Williams, LF
Jimmie Foxx, 1B	Jimmie Foxx, 1B
Bobby Doerr, 2B	Nomar Garciaparra, SS
Carlton Fisk, C	Carlton Fisk, C
Dwight Evans, RF	Dwight Evans, RF
Frank Malzone (or Wade Boggs), 3B	Frank Malzone, 3B
Pedro Martinez, RHP	Lefty Grove, LHP
Mel Parnell, LHP	Pedro Martinez, RHP
Dick Radatz Reliever	Dick Radatz, Reliever

 When Johnny Pesky signed with the Red Sox out of high school in 1940, little did he know that he had found a virtual lifetime employer. Except for brief detours through the Detroit and Washington organizations in the 1950s, Pesky has been drawing a paycheck from the Red Sox regularly for more than six decades. As the 21st century dawned, he was an octogenarian instructor in the organization.

Pesky, a shortstop and third baseman, played brilliantly for the Red Sox for seven years. He led the American League in hits in each of his first three seasons and ended his major league career as a .307 hitter. Pesky managed the Red Sox in 1963 and 1964, was a Red Sox coach for a decade, and has held positions in the team's minor-league and scouting departments.

Having witnessed more than 60 years of Red Sox baseball, Pesky doesn't need to research an all-time Red Sox team; he ate, slept and drank with most of the Red Sox greats.

 Nobody — not even Johnny Pesky — has been around the Red Sox longer than Charlie Wagner, who signed with the club in 1935 and entered the 2005 season as baseball's only 92-year-old special assignment instructor. Wagner's longevity earned him the honor of throwing out the ceremonial first pitch at a May 2001 game commemorating the 100th anniversary of the franchise. "It was a nice feeling to be there with all those guys," he says. "I cried through half of it. I now cry at the weather report, too."

Wagner had a modest major league career. He pitched in six seasons for the Red Sox, going 32-23 in the 1930s and 1940s. Perhaps Wagner's great claim to fame was being Ted Williams' road roommate — "Ted was a good roomy; early to bed, early to rise, and he talked baseball morning to night." Wagner left the Red Sox's active roster after the 1946 season and became a lifer in the team's minor-league and scouting departments. Like Pesky, Wagner can draw on a lifetime of memories to select an all-time Red Sox team.

MO VAUGHN

JIMMIE FOXX

JOHNNY PESKY I have to pick Jimmie Foxx. I played only two months with Foxx when I got here in 1942. He was losing his eyesight, but everyone knew what he could do. Ted Williams used to talk about some of Jimmie's long home runs. My rookie year we'd go into Detroit, Chicago, St. Louis, Washington or New York, and Ted would say, "Foxx hit one there, and he also hit one there," pointing out the farthest reaches of the stands. Ted said of his era, of his time, Foxx hit balls as far as anyone did. He hit one in the third deck in Yankee Stadium. I think he's one of only five players to slug over .600 lifetime (.609). Foxx was built like a tank. He was a wonderful man, smoked a cigar, and had a great way about him. Mo Vaughn could hit too. George Scott was good, but not as good overall as Vaughn. Vaughn was Boston.

CHARLIE WAGNER Foxx is my pick, too. He could hit, run, he had one of the greatest arms in baseball, and he was a delightful man. You want distance home runs? He hit one out in New York off Lefty Gomez; it landed in the third deck. Years later Gomez said, "You know that unidentified white object we discovered on the moon? It was that homer Foxx hit off me." I had dinner with Foxx any number of times. He could drink, but nothing to excess. Every day he was on that ballfield and ready to go.

JIMMIE FOXX

ALL-TIME LEADERS

SLUGGING

BABE RUTH	.690
TED WILLIAMS	.634
LOU GEHRIG	.632
TODD HELTON	.618*
BARRY BONDS	.611*
JIMMIE FOXX	.609
HANK GREENBERG	.605
MANNY RAMIREZ	.599*
VLADIMIR GUERRERO	.589*
MARK McGWIRE	.588

HOME RUNS

HANK AARON	755
BABE RUTH	714
BARRY BONDS	703*
WILLIE MAYS	660
FRANK ROBINSON	586
MARK McGWIRE	583
SAMMY SOSA	574*
HARMON KILLEBREW	573
REGGIE JACKSON	563
RAFAEL PALMEIRO	551*
MIKE SCHMIDT	548
MICKEY MANTLE	536
JIMMIE FOXX	534

RBI

HANK AARON	2,297
BABE RUTH	2,213
CAP ANSON	2,076
LOU GEHRIG	1,995
STAN MUSIAL	1,951
TY COBB	1,937
JIMMIE FOXX	1,921
WILLIE MAYS	1,903
MEL OTT	1,861

*Through 2004 season

BOBBY DOERR

Bobby Doerr belongs at second. He was a great player, one of the better players of my era. He hit home runs, played very well overall. Doerr had a great World Series in 1946 — he hit .409. During the pennant race in 1948 he had something like 400 straight chances without an error (Doerr handled 414 consecutive errorless chances from June 24 through September 19). Joe McCarthy came to manage the Red Sox in 1948, and he loved Joe Gordon, who had been his second baseman in New York. But he also liked Bobby.

Doerr could do everything. He could make that second end of the double play — nobody was better. He had a little glove, and fielded as well as anyone. He was in the twilight of his career when I first came up, but still a real good player.

NOMAR GARCIAPARRA
JOE CRONIN

 I take Nomar Garciaparra, though I liked Rico Petrocelli because he hit a lot of home runs. I think Petrocelli was the first American League shortstop to hit 40 homers in a year—and he was a good all-around player. I liked Rick Burleson and Luis Aparicio, too. But Garciaparra can do it all: steal a base, hit a homer, play the field, and he's led the league in hitting. On fielding alone, I would pick Aparicio. Joe Cronin was a great hitter, but he was winding down his career when I came up. He was a player-manager and usually just pinch-hit. Then he turned the managing over to me.

 Cronin and Garciaparra. Cronin was a tough two-strike hitter. Didn't bother him one damn bit to hit with two strikes on him. Garciaparra is everything you want in an offensive player, and he's as good at defense as there has ever been. He has a great arm.

WADE BOGGS

JOHNNY PESKY I see only two people: Wade Boggs and Frank Malzone. Boggs was selected for the Hall of Fame. He had 200 hits and 100 walks in the same season four times. Only Lou Gehrig did it more — seven times. Boggs was what you call a pure hitter. He could handle the bat as well as anyone who's ever played the game. He was like a great violinist, a virtuoso with a bat in his hands. He kept in shape and he spent a lot of time practicing — I always admired him because he worked so hard. I hit him grounders every day, and he worked at becoming a good fielder. Malzone was a great fielder, had power, and played hard.

CHARLIE WAGNER I take Malzone. He was one of the great fielders. He was a great help to Boggs when Boggs first came up — he helped him no end on learning how to play third base. The hitting part, Boggs didn't need any help. For his type hitter, there was nobody to match him. And he could have been a home run hitter if he wanted to. Except for Ted Williams, I can't recall anybody who could put the bat on the ball as often as Boggs did and hit it as solidly. Boggs was hitting .300 every year in the minor leagues. The reason they kept him in the minor leagues for four or five years is that he couldn't catch a ball.

FRANK MALZONE

Carlton Fisk is the best catcher we ever had. He worked hard at it, and he deserved everything he got. He'd go through all those mannerisms at the plate — you'd think he was in pain and coming apart at the seams. But he was a gamer, and he'd come through for you in the clutch.

Fisk is my choice, too, and I have another guy named Moe Berg. Fisk came fast. I had him as a kid when he first came to spring training with the big club. He didn't have a glove, and as he walked by I said, "Hey young man, where's your glove? What position do you play?" He said, "I play catcher. I thought they gave you gloves here." The Rawlings glove people were there, and I said, "You'd better go get yourself a glove" — and that's probably the best advice I ever had for him. The

pitchers liked to throw to him because he didn't miss any balls. He didn't do anything stupid. He just had a real presence on the field.

Berg couldn't hit too well, but he was a pitcher's catcher. They're always asking if a catcher can hit — that isn't always the thing. The game starts when the pitcher throws the ball. And that's where a good catcher makes the whole story. A pitcher has a good feeling about a catcher that looks as big as the building he's in. Berg was one of those guys.

TED WILLIAMS

JOHNNY PESKY I'd have to pick a couple of guys at each position. Ted Williams, of course, and Yaz in left. Dom DiMaggio and Fred Lynn in center, and Dwight Evans in right.

Ted would take a lot of batting practice, and he'd do a lot of hitting on an off day. He was always swinging a bat, and he had such a great mind. When we were just kids on the Red Sox, we all lived at the Sheraton Hotel on the river in Boston. Ted had a big mirror in his room, and he'd stand in front of it and look at his swing. For a guy that young, blessed with all that talent, he really worked to take advantage of it

When I hit in front of Ted, I never got to hit 2-and-0 or 3-and-1. I had to take, hoping I could get a walk, because we never wanted Williams leading off an inning. I used to get brushed with pitches just to get him up to the plate. One time I came into the dugout after grounding to second on a 3-and-1 pitch and I said to nobody in particular, "Why don't I get to hit 2-and-0 and 3-and-1 more often." Our manager Joe McCarthy heard me and said, "As long as you're here, you'll do as you're told." I felt like a nickel. I went to see him after the game and I said, "Joe, I'm sorry." He said "I understand your frustration, but we've got the best hitter in baseball." I thought McCarthy was the smartest man I ever played for.

I remember in 1946 we got off to a great start. Dom DiMaggio was hitting .400, I was hitting .400, and Williams was hitting .500. Bobby Doerr was hitting behind Ted, and Bobby was hitting about .260. We were about 30 or 40 games into the season, and one day before batting practice, Bobby, Dom and me were in the dugout talking and here comes Ted. He says to Doerr, "For crying out loud, you got your hands up here, down here, open stance, closed stance, feet together — get a good stance and give it a try." Bobby said to him, "Ted, I'm not you." Williams threw his arms up and said, "You want to be a lousy .280 hitter, be a lousy .280 hitter." Doerr went on to knock in 116 runs that year. That was Ted — a real perfectionist when it came to hitting.

Yaz, by the time he was 25 years old, was a complete player. At first he was kind of a wild swinger. But he could hit, and he had great baseball instincts. I've heard Dick Williams say that if he had to take one year for someone who was most outstanding in everything he did, he would take Yaz in 1967. That year Yaz would hit a homer in the late innings if we were one or two runs down, or he would make a great catch, or throw someone out whatever it took. I managed Yaz in 1963 and 1964. I was energetic and young, and I felt good about managing for the club I grew up with. I made a couple of suggestions to Yaz, and he kind of barked at me a little bit. Maybe my tone of voice wasn't what it could have been. I learned from that; I found out you don't bother the good players. My first year, he was at the plate with a man on third with one out, and he decided to bunt on his own. I said, "Carl, you're our best player. I'm depending on you to hit the ball. You might hit one out of the ballpark. I don't want you bunting. It would be like asking Ted Williams to bunt." I ruffled his feathers a little bit.

And let's not forget Jim Rice, one of my all-time favorites. He was a terrific hitter, so strong, power to all fields. Rice really worked at learning how to play the Wall. I hit him a lot of balls off the Wall, line drives, on the ground — and he never had enough. He'd say, "Come on Woody (short for Woodpecker, Pesky's nickname), let's go." When he first got here, he threw sidearm, but when he realized that if you throw over the top, the ball wouldn't tail, it would

go straight, he wound up leading the league in assists for outfielders.

 If you have to pick one, it's Williams. He was a great teammate, and he was one of the all-time perfectionists. If he put his mind to it, there wasn't anything he couldn't do better than the other guy. He didn't try to impress anyone; he just wanted to be the best at the things that were important to him. For example, he was nuts about fishing, and he became a great fisherman. I went with him once in Cleveland to see a guy who made flies for fishing for a living. Ted showed the guy some of the flies he had made, and the guy said, "You make them better than I do."

Yastrzemski was a leader. He was the leader of the band, like a Joe DiMaggio, one of those type guys. You couldn't wait until Yaz got to bat. He could really help you in the outfield, too, especially playing balls off the Green Monster. Any ball he could get to he could catch, and he had a pretty good arm. Yaz held his bat very high when he came up, and Williams told him, "We aren't going to do any changing now, but some day we're gonna bring that bat down and you'll be in position to hit." Before you know it, Yaz did bring his bat down.

FRED LYNN

JIM RICE

JOHNNY PESKY I wasn't born when Tris Speaker played for the Red Sox, so I can't tell you about him first-hand. I played with Dom DiMaggio, and I was told that he and Speaker where similar in the way they played a very shallow center field. Dom is the only outfielder to have an unassisted double play in the World Series, and I believe he had 35 assists one year. He was a leadoff man, too; he hit .300 four or five times.

The best outfield we ever had around here was Rice, Lynn, and Evans. Lynn was great — he could really go get the ball, and he had power.

CHARLIE WAGNER Dom DiMaggio — no one was any better in center field. He had a great arm, and played like a shortstop. When he was in a big outfield, you could really see how good he was. He got to a ball quicker than any man I've ever seen. Lynn came up in 1975 and played like he'd been here forever. Power, hitting for average, good arm — he had it all.

1931

CENTER FIELD
CF

Dwight Evans was a big, good-looking guy, about 6-foot-3, looked like Rock Hudson. He could hit, run and throw-just a helluva player. He hit almost 400 home runs.

Evans is the best right fielder we've ever had, no question. I had him as a kid in the minors in Corning, New York, and it was just a treat to watch everything he could do. He had a great arm, and he took real pleasure in throwing the ball accurately.

DWIGHT EVANS

JOHNNY PESKY

Roger Clemens is as good a pitcher as I've ever seen. To me he's the best pitcher the Red Sox ever had, although you'll probably get some argument from others on that. Cy Young was well before my time, but you gotta include him. The rest of my starting five is Pedro Martinez, Mel Parnell, and Ted Hughson. My reliever is Dick Radatz.

We all know how great Pedro is. Parnell was a stylish lefthander, a great pitcher. Hughson won 20, and he came up lame. We had other good ones here, too. Boo Ferris won 21 in 1945, his first year with us, and 25 the next year, but he had an asthmatic condition. One day in Chicago in 95-degree heat, he kept having to use the inhaler he carried in his pocket, but he still went nine innings. A real tough kid. Mickey Harris and Joe Dobson showed real promise, but they both came up lame, too.

PITCHER P

LEFTY GROVE

CHARLIE WAGNER

Lefty Grove is my No. 1 starter. He was the toughest loser I've ever seen. When he was pitching, he was the boss — give me the damn ball, get out of my way. I never saw anyone with a better pitching motion than Lefty. He threw over the top and down through — I have movies of him. His movement is so perfect it's unreal.

Martinez is my second starter. He's really rough, and he throws all the pitches well. Clemens is next. He would take the ball whenever you gave it to him. He was like Grove; he wanted to let the hitter know how fast he was. He could throw unbelievably hard, and his ball had great movement. Luis Tiant is my fourth starter, then I take Parnell. In the bullpen, I liked Radatz and Bob Stanley. Radatz had a curveball that would knock you down.

I met Cy Young in Toledo when I was a kid in 1937. They were honoring him that day, and he went to the mound and threw for about five minutes. I never saw anyone who was as loose as he was at age 60. My manager Donie Bush played with Young, and he said Young was as fluid as anyone was. Herb Pennock, who was my pitching coach in Boston, played with Babe Ruth and told me how great he was. Ruth didn't work at being good, but he was good. He liked to hit better than he liked to pitch.

[BOTTOM ROW LEFT TO RIGHT] >

TEX HUGHSON
DICK RADATZ
MEL PARNELL

I wasn't born when Tris Speaker played for the Red Sox, so I can't tell you about him first-hand. I played with Dom DiMaggio, and I was told that he and Speaker where similar in the way they played a very shallow center field. Dom is the only outfielder to have an unassisted double play in the World Series, and I believe he had 35 assists one year. He was a leadoff man, too; he hit .300 four or five times.

The best outfield we ever had around here was Rice, Lynn, and Evans. Lynn was great — he could really go get the ball, and he had power.

Dom DiMaggio — no one was any better in center field. He had a great arm, and played like a shortstop. When he was in a big outfield, you could really see how good he was. He got to a ball quicker than any man I've ever seen. Lynn came up in 1975 and played like he'd been here forever. Power, hitting for average, good arm — he had it all.

1931

Dwight Evans was a big, good-looking guy, about 6-foot-3, looked like Rock Hudson. He could hit, run and throw-just a helluva player. He hit almost 400 home runs.

Evans is the best right fielder we've ever had, no question. I had him as a kid in the minors in Corning, New York, and it was just a treat to watch everything he could do. He had a great arm, and he took real pleasure in throwing the ball accurately.

DWIGHT EVANS

ROGER CLEMENS

Between them, **Charlie Wagner** and **Johnny Pesky** have played with or seen every big league player since the 1930s. But a few of the greatest Red Sox players predated even them, including the pitcher **BABE RUTH, CY YOUNG, HARRY HOOPER, JIMMY COLLINS** and **TRIS SPEAKER, HALL OF FAMERS EVERY ONE.** Here then are the players who might have been chosen at their respective Red Sox positions had Charlie and Johnny seen these players in their prime.

RUTH
AS A PITCHER
IN HIS FIRST THREE FULL SEASONS
1915 - 1916 - 1917

65 WINS
33 LOSSES

67 VICTORIES BY AGE
23

2.02 ERA

ONLY THREE PITCHERS IN THE 20th CENTURY WON MORE GAMES THAN RUTH BY AGE 23:

BOB FELLER	107
SMOKY JOE WOOD	81
DWIGHT GOODEN	73

Clearly Babe Ruth's accomplishments present a compelling case for him as the greatest hitter who ever lived. But there can be no argument that he was the greatest player ever, based on one simple fact: Given a chance, Ruth also might have become one of the game's great pitchers. Consider this: In his first three seasons, before he began the transition to outfielder, Ruth posted a record of 65-33 with a 2.02 ERA. The ERA was the fourth best in the majors during those three seasons (1915-1917) and he ranked third in victories during that span behind a pair of high-end Hall of Famers: Grover Cleveland Alexander (94-35) and Walter Johnson (75-49).

By the time he turned 23, Ruth had earned 67 victories. Only three pitchers in the 20th century won more games by that age: Bob Feller (107), Smoky Joe Wood (81) and Dwight Gooden (73).

Generations later, it's difficult to appreciate the magnitude of Ruth's unprecedented hitting achievements, at least as they were viewed by his contemporaries. Perhaps only in recent years, as Mark McGwire, Sammy Sosa and Barry Bonds stretched the limits of what many once considered possible, have we seen anything to help put Ruth in that context. But combined with what Ruth did as a pitcher, and the unrealized potential that it implied, there really is nothing before or after to compare.

P PITCHER

116 WINS

57 LOSSES

20 WINS OR MORE IN

1911 AND 1912

WOOD

14 SEASONS
1908-1915 WITH THE RED SOX

2.03 ERA

Nobody threw harder than Smoky Joe Wood, a fact acknowledged by even the great Walter Johnson. "Can I throw harder than Joe Wood? Mister, there's no man alive can throw hard than Joe Wood," Johnson told a sports writer in 1912. The 5-foot-11, 180-pound Wood enjoyed one of the greatest seasons ever by a pitcher in 1912, going 34-5 with 35 complete games and 10 shutouts, then winning three games in the World Series as the Red Sox beat the New York Giants. For good measure, Wood batted .290 in 1912. On September 6, 1912, the 22-year-old Wood and the 24-year-old Johnson engaged in one of baseball's all-time classic pitching matchups. Wood, working on a 14-game winning streak, beat Johnson

and the Washington Senators, 1-0, in a game pitched so efficiently that it was over in just 106 minutes. Wood's streak would reach 16, tying a major league record that Johnson had set earlier in the season. The following spring, Wood slipped on wet grass while fielding a ground ball and suffered a broken right thumb. When he was able to pitch again, he could not throw without experiencing pain in his right shoulder. Wood persevered and pitched for the Red Sox for three more seasons, even going 15-5 and leading the American League in ERA (1.49) in 1915. The pain, though, drove him out of baseball for a year, and when he returned he soon gave up pitching and completed his career as an outfielder with the Cleveland Indians.

20 wins or more 16 times, 30 wins or more five times

| 22 seasons, including 1901-1908 with the Red Sox | 14 seasons, Including 1901-1907 with the Red Sox |

YOUNG *Cy*

COLLINS *Jimmy*

PITCHER

511-313 » 2.63 ERA

HALL OF FAME » 1937

THIRD BASE

.294 » 64 HR » 982 RBIs

HALL OF FAME » 1945

By the time he joined the Red Sox in 1901, Cy Young had won 285 games and pitched more than 4,000 innings — numbers that would indicate a fabulous career for 99 percent of the pitchers who have worked in the major leagues. Young was 34 at the time, and in his eight years in Boston he would win another 193 games on his way to 511 career victories — 94 more than any other pitcher in history. Remarkably, Young might have had more victories, but he grew into a portly man and opponents seized on the opportunity to regularly bunt successfully against him. So he was forced into retirement at age 44, without so much as a twinge of pain in a remarkable right arm that churned out 7,356 innings — 1,415 more than any other pitcher in history. Young attributed his good health to an offseason regime of chopping wood and doing heavy chores on his Ohio farm. Born Denton True Young, he gained his nickname from a catcher who warmed him up when he tried out for the Canton, Ohio, minor league team. The catcher told sports writers Young threw "as fast as a cyclone." So he became Cy, a pitcher with records that likely will forever remain unchallenged.

Jimmy Collins was the Red Sox's first manager and their first star player. He jumped to the team for its inaugural season in 1901 after being offered more money than Boston's National League club, the Braves, would pay him. Collins had no peer among third basemen until Pie Traynor came along in the 1920s. Sturdily built at 5-foot-8 and 160 pounds, Collins was a fine hitter (better than .300 five times) and had above-average power for his day. While he was a true asset at the plate, his value soared once he took his defensive position. Sure-handed and ultra-quick, Collins was a master at fielding bunts, which were a frequent offensive ploy in the dead-ball era. He holds the National League record for chances by a third baseman in a season (601 in 1899) and ranks second all-time at his position in career putouts. Collins was the Red Sox's manager for six years, including the pennant-winning seasons of 1903 and 1904. The Red Sox won the first World Series, in 1903, but there was no Series in 1904 because the leagues were feuding. Collins was traded to the Philadelphia Athletics in 1908 and was out of baseball by 1911. He was inducted into the Hall of Fame in 1945, two years after his death at age 69 in his native Buffalo, New York.

22 seasons, including 1907-15 with the Red Sox

17 seasons, including 1909-1920 with the Red Sox

SPEAKER *Tris*

HOOPER *Harry*

CENTER FIELD

.344 » 117 HR » 1,881 RBIs

HALL OF FAME » 1937

RIGHT FIELD

.281 » 75 HR » 817 RBIs

HALL OF FAME » 1971

By most accounts, Tris Speaker was one of the top 10 players among those in the major leagues during the first half of the 20th century. His plaque in the Hall of Fame describes him as the greatest center fielder of his day. From 1910 to 1915, Speaker, Harry Hooper and Duffy Lewis formed the Red Sox's famed "Million Dollar Outfield." One of the fastest players of his era, Speaker played shallow in center field, daring batters to try and hit the ball over his head; they rarely did. The 6-foot, 195-pound Speaker had a powerful swing from the left side of the plate that rained line drives to all fields. More than 75 years after he ceased playing, he remains the all-time major league leader for doubles (792). Hugely popular in Boston, Speaker was one of the first athletes to cash in on his celebrity. He received $50 each time he hit the Bull Durham sign at Fenway Park, endorsed Boston Garters, had a $2 straw hat named in his honor, and received free clothing from manufacturers. The Texas-born Speaker would have been content to spend his career in Boston if not for the slight he felt when Red Sox owner Joe Lannin attempted to cut his salary to less than $10,000 after the club won the 1915 World Series. Lannin cited Speaker's batting average, which had fallen for four straight seasons. Speaker refused to sign and was traded to the Cleveland Indians, who benefited from his .354 batting average over the next 11 seasons. It was the second time the Red Sox had infuriated Speaker. Trying to make the team as a 20-year-old in 1908, he did not fare well in spring training and was left behind in Little Rock, Arkansas, as payment for the use of the training camp.

Although he was a fine ballplayer as part of the Red Sox's "Million Dollar Outfield" with Tris Speaker and Duffy Lewis, Harry Hooper is best-remembered for his part in Babe Ruth leaving the pitcher's mound for full-time work as a hitter. As the story goes, the erudite Hooper — he was a college man — convinced Red Sox manager Ed Barrow that as great as the young Ruth was on the mound, he had even more promise as a hitter. Barrow agreed to let Ruth play in the outfield on the days he didn't pitch. The left-handed batting Hooper was the Red Sox's leadoff hitter and right fielder from 1909 through 1920. He got on base more than 40 percent of the time and ran the bases better than any of his teammates. When he left the Red Sox, he was the club's all-time leader in triples (130) and stolen bases (300). Hooper was an innovator in the outfield, developing the rump slide to catch short fly balls that became widely copied, and he had a rifle for an arm. The California native was inducted into the Hall of Fame in 1971 and he died three years later at age 87.

1967

AQUARIUS DAWNED, BOSTON ROCKED AND ALL HELL BROKE LOOSE

5

THE MOON WAS IN THE SEVENTH HOUSE.

Yaz batted third.

JUPITER ALIGNED WITH MARS.

Lonborg faced Chance.

PEACE GUIDED THE PLANETS.

BUT ROXBURY BURNED, AND VIETNAM WAS DEATH.

Dick Williams raged.

In 1967, Aquarius dawned, Boston rocked and all hell broke loose. More American soldiers died in Vietnam by the end of September — 6,721 — than during the previous six years. Heavyweight champion Muhammad Ali was stripped of his title for refusing a draft notice. Israel repulsed Arab armies in a six-day war. Former Harvard professor Timothy Leary preached the virtue of hallucinogenic drugs. Yale undergraduate Bill Clinton smoked pot but didn't inhale. Jimi Hendrix lit his Fender Stratocaster on fire at the Monterey Pop Festival. Black ghettos ignited with frustration and rage. The Beatles meditated with Maharishi Mahesh Yogi while flower children went to San Francisco for a Summer of Love. Martin Luther King Jr. and Bobby Kennedy were alive, and so were J. Edgar Hoover and George Wallace. Richard Nixon was planning his comeback, LBJ his exit.

And the Red Sox won the pennant.

It was pennant befitting 1967, a 500-year-flood of a pennant, a pennant so frenetic and outlandish and magical it was dubbed "The Impossible Dream" after a song in a then-popular Broadway musical about Don Quixote. And really, what better imagery to describe those 100-to-1-shot Red Sox, a group that tilted at windmills and won.

Four teams — Boston, Minnesota, Chicago and Detroit — entered the final week separated by 1½ games. It ended on the final evening of the final day, with the Red Sox glued to a clubhouse radio, listening as the California Angels eliminated the Tigers in the second game of a doubleheader at Detroit.

Power to the people of Red Sox Nation!

Nobody gave the Red Sox a chance, except perhaps the 8,324 fans who showed up for Opening Day at Fenway Park for a 5-4 win over the White Sox. By the middle of the summer, and in ensuing years as attendance swelled toward 1.7 million, 8,324 would seem as

1967 >

01.03.67

> Jack Ruby, assassin of Lee Harvey Oswald, dies at the age of 55.

| 104 |

obsolete as the dreary era preceding it. From 1960 through 1966 the Red Sox lost 125 games more than they won and never finished higher than sixth place. In 1965 they were ninth with a 62-100 record, and in 1966 they were ninth again at 72-90 with home attendance of 811,172. The Red Sox were called everything in those days, including selfish, lazy and spoiled. But Red Sox owner Tom Yawkey set a new direction in late 1965 with the promotion of his business manager, Dick O'Connell, to general manager. In turn, O'Connell hired a rookie manager, Dick Williams, to lead the charge into 1967.

The 37-year-old Williams became the second-youngest manager in the major leagues, and probably the most surly and sarcastic. Crewcut and authoritarian, he was the drill sergeant nightmare of every hippie, and the scourge of laid-back baseball. Having ended his journeyman

career on the 1963 and 1964 Boston squads, Williams was on to the tricks of his former teammates. "They knew what I knew," Williams says. "They had been goofing off and stealing Mr. Yawkey's money." Williams motivated with the spur and whip — what he couldn't accomplish with criticism and threats he did with fines and benchings. He lumped players together with umpires, reporters and league officials — treating them all the same, which was badly.

In his 1990 autobiography, *No More Mr. Nice Guy*, Williams recounted his hardscrabble St. Louis childhood and a tough-as-nails but oft-unemployed father. Williams learned to swim when his father tossed him in the rushing current of an Ozark river, ordered him to stroke, and stood behind him while the current forced him downstream. This harsh upbringing shaped his managing, Williams wrote, because "my competitive fire, kindled in me during those days of learning to swim upstream in a Missouri river, became a continuous rolling explosion. If we lost and we'd done everything right, I'd try to understand. It would be painful but I'd try. But if we lost because one person had made a mental mistake, I'd blow up. Sometimes right on the spot, even before the game was won or lost — if I thought somebody didn't care as much as I did, I'd damn near kill him."

In February 1967, this was the authoritative personality confronting a group of players described by a newspaper reporter as "a pack of rookies, misfits, castoffs and Carl Yastrzemski." Surely pitcher Jim Lonborg, first baseman George Scott, second baseman Mike Andrews, shortstop Rico Petrocelli, and outfielders Tony Conigliaro and Reggie Smith merited greater respect. But the basic premise was sound — Yastrzemski was lead dog. A six-year veteran and former batting champion, Yaz was a good player falling short of

> Albert DeSalvo, the Boston Strangler,
is sentenced to life in prison.

01.18.67

01.23.67

The Red Sox report they have received an offer of $500,000 from the Athletics for 22-year-old outfielder Tony Conigliaro.

DALTON JONES

greatness. His outward lack of emotion occasionally appeared like nonchalance, and his close relationship with Yawkey had cut the legs out from under a couple of managers.

Moving quickly to assert control, Williams stripped Yaz of his captaincy and replaced him with…himself. Henceforth there would be no captain, Williams announced, because anyone with a problem or complaint could bring it to him directly. The unspoken message was that everyone from star to journeyman would be treated alike. (How iconoclastic was the manager? Early in spring training another Williams — the legendary Ted — showed up, as he had routinely since his retirement, to lecture on the finer points of the game. When Ted disagreed with some of Dick's methods, specifically having pitchers play volleyball to improve their eye-hand coordination, Dick told Ted to stay away from his pitchers and his pitchers to stay away from Ted; soon, Ted stayed away from Dick, packed up and left.)

Williams set up a weight chart and instituted daily weigh-ins. (This proved to be a season-long problem for the plumpish Scott, an avid and capable eater, until Williams finally benched him for a three-game series with the Angels in August. From then on, Scott made his weight.) When two players showed up late for a spring training workout, Williams publicly berated them and ordered the team hotel to call the rooms of all players at 7 a.m. each day. Training camp was a refresher course on fundamentals —

principles Williams had learned coming up in the Los Angeles Dodgers system. "Right from the start you could see he meant business," Petrocelli says. "He got on people for mental mistakes. He could tolerate an error, but not a mental mistake. You had to be in the game."

Williams also could delegate authority judiciously. Petrocelli, the third-year shortstop, had lost his confidence under the previous manager, Billy Herman. Williams set about restoring it by telling Petrocelli he was in charge of the young infield of third baseman Joe Foy, second baseman Mike Andrews and Scott. "If you want to move these guys around, you don't have to ask me," Williams told Petrocelli.

"I like it," the shortstop replied. The ripple effect had Andrews, a rookie, improving under Petrocelli's guidance. "I had only played one season at second in the minors," Andrews says. "But Rico was so steady he made it work."

A disciplined and businesslike club opened the season, and in the third game an omen was delivered. Rookie lefthander Billy Rohr came within one out of pitching a no-hitter against the New York Yankees at Yankee Stadium. Yastrzemski kept it alive with a spectacular tumbling catch of a Tom Tresh smash to open the ninth, but with two out Elston Howard lined a clean single to right. Rohr pocketed the one-hit 3-0 shutout, and even though he won just one more game and faded back to the minors, his cameo was a precursor to the Impossible Dream.

> U.S. troops begin largest offensive of the Vietnam War.

02.23.67

03.06.67

03.31.67

> Teamster boss Jimmy Hoffa enters Lewisburg Federal Prison.

> In London, Jimi Hendrix sets his guitar on fire for the first time.

1967 BATTING AVERAGE

.303

RUNS

74

DOUBLES

21

GEORGE [**BOOMER**] SCOTT

HOME RUNS

19

RBI

82

FIELDING PERCENTAGE

.987

"If I thought somebody didn't care as much as I did, I'd damn near kill him."

DICK WILLIAMS

As April and May unfolded, Williams was unrelenting, not only with his players, but with umpires. Slumping players — among them Yastrzemski, Smith, Scott and Foy — were benched. Yawkey, whose presence in the clubhouse Williams viewed as subversive, was given the cold shoulder. Williams' baiting of umpires was obsessive and nasty — in one game he argued with umpires at first base, second, third and home plate. Yet the manager's aggressiveness transformed righthander Jim Lonborg, whose long hair and Stanford pedigree reflected a genteel manner on the mound, as did his 19-27 career record. Williams ordered Lonborg to pitch inside and to use his hard sinking fastball in tight situations. In a May game against the Angels, Lonborg took a 1-0 lead into the bottom of the ninth and blew it, 2-1, trying to finesse batters. "As Jim is walking off, Rico Petrocelli patted him on the back and said 'nice game' to bolster him," says Red Sox radio broadcaster Ken Coleman. "Dick Williams overheard it and said, 'Nice game, my ass.'"

Lonborg got the message. In June, after Foy was beaned by the Yankees' Thad Tillotson, Lonborg drilled Tillotson in the shoulder, inciting a brawl. When Lonborg came to bat, Tillotson plunked him, and the clubs brawled again. Lonborg retaliated by hitting Dick Howser in the back, clearing the benches a third time. Williams and Yankees manager Ralph Houk were threatened with suspensions, but Williams was exhilarated. "In that one incident, [Lonborg] had

> New Zealander Dave McKenzie wins the Boston Marathon, setting a course record of 2:15:45.

04.14.67   04.19.67

At Yankee Stadium, lefthander Billy Rohr makes his major league debut for the Red Sox, no-hitting New York for 8⅔ innings.

[110]

proved to me and to the rest of the league that he wasn't going to be just another frightened kid with talent — he was going to be a scary kid with talent," Williams wrote.

With the unwanted burden of being captain lifted, Yaz set about finding his inner Hall of Famer. Batting coach Bobby Doerr got Yaz to hold his bat high, and with his new stance he was consistently able to turn on the ball and pull it high and deep to right. In June, White Sox manager Eddie Stanky commented that Yaz was an All-Star "from the neck down." In a doubleheader the following day Yaz went 6-for-9 and homered in his final at-bat. As he headed for home Yaz tipped his cap to Stanky. Of Williams, Yastrzemski later would say, "He was the right guy at the time. He was young, aggressive, full of fire. Personally, I liked him. I know what he was trying to do. But he might have been a little harsh at times."

By the end of May, the Red Sox were two games above .500 and not yet a contender. O'Connell made a couple of smart moves in early June, acquiring utility infielder Jerry Adair from the White Sox and righthander Gary Bell from the Cleveland Indians. Also in June, Conigliaro stunned the White Sox, 2-1, with a two-out, two-run home run on a 3-and-2 pitch in the bottom of the 11th; at the end of the month Boston was three games over .500, 5½ games behind Chicago. At the All-Star break, the Sox were six games out. The break provided a barometer. The reborn Lonborg, who had mounted a 10-2 record, and Yastrzemski, Petrocelli and Conigliaro went to the midsummer classic. "About halfway through the year we realized, 'Hey, there's no one better than us out there,'" Andrews says. "We had so many young guys. Once we'd been around the league we knew how good we were."

After the break the Red Sox jelled dramatically, winning 10 in a row, improving to 52-40 and pulling to within a half-game of the White Sox. Arriving back at Boston's Logan Airport on July 23, the Sox were greeted by 10,000 madly screaming fans — more than had attended Opening Day. "You'd have thought the Beatles landed," Petrocelli says. Fans and players mingled at the baggage carousel, floating on a cloud of baseball euphoria. That moment may pinpoint the birth of modern Red Sox Nation. New England throbbed with pennant fever. Ken Coleman's children were at crowded Nantasket Beach on a steamy Sunday afternoon when the Sox fell behind the Angels, 8-0. Thousands of transistor radios crackled as the Sox mounted a comeback. Adair won the game, 9-8, with a home run. "My kids told me the beach erupted — a hundred thousand people were screaming," Coleman says.

They were dancing on Nantasket Beach, and in the streets, and all along the watchtower. The pulse of Red Sox Nation quickened.

04.28.67

> **Muhammad Ali is stripped of his boxing title after refusing induction into the Army.**

[PUTOUTS + ASSISTS] ÷ [PUTOUTS + ASSISTS + ERRORS] =

.970

1967 FIELDING PERCENTAGE [RICO PETROCELLI]

Yet baseball's bubble existence could not keep out the larger world. The Red Sox often shared Page One with stark headlines:

19 Year Olds First, Draft Chief Says

Four players — Lonborg, Conigliaro, Dalton Jones and Jim Landis — were called for two-week stints with their reserve military units. Letters from Vietnam routinely arrived in the clubhouse. Soldiers were listening to Red Sox broadcasts on Armed Forces Radio. "I pray to God I live long enough to see you guys win the pennant," wrote a soldier. Petrocelli shudders remembering those letters. "We were aware of what was happening," he says. "We were concerned." Andrews visited wounded soldiers recuperating at a military hospital in the Charlestown neighborhood of Boston. "This chaotic war was going on while we were playing baseball," Andrews says. "To think that baseball could be meaningful to these wounded soldiers was unbelievable."

Early in June came another headline:

Police Battle Rioters in Roxbury

Boston's poorest and blackest neighborhood erupted in flames. A firefighter was shot in the wrist by a sniper. Detroit was rioting when the Red Sox arrived for a three-game series. "There was shooting down the street from Tiger Stadium," Petrocelli says. "We took the bus from the ballpark to the hotel. We couldn't go out of the hotel." America was tearing apart at the seams. Or was it simply molting a cancerous skin?

Within baseball itself a revolution was sprouting. A new and aggressive executive director of the Major League Baseball Players Association, Marvin Miller, was setting his sights on the feudal control exercised by owners. With the overturning of the illegal reserve clause his ultimate objective — to be achieved in 1975 — Miller pushed for improvements in pension benefits, minimum salary and working conditions. Documenting the embryonic union movement in 1967, author John Helyar wrote that one player representative, pitcher Milt Pappas, even spoke up for the growing ranks of players abandoning crewcuts for the mod look. "There aren't enough outlets for hair dryers in the clubhouses," Pappas complained.

05.01.67

> Singer Elvis Presley weds Priscilla Ann Beaulieu in Las Vegas.

05.05.67

Facing the Orioles' Eddie Fisher at Fenway Park, Carl Yastrzemski hits his 100th career home run.

Sub-Culture of Hippies Linked to Red Threat in U.S.

A gathering of ultra-conservatives calling itself the New England Rally for God, Family and Country met at Boston's Statler Hilton. The organizer proclaimed that "the breakdown of law and order, emergence of narcotics as a significant peril, burgeoning of the New Left on campuses and folk songs and folk singers, are all tied to a breakdown of morality and faith effected by communists in America." A culture was emerging, all right, and some rushed to embrace it. A new publication, Avant Garde Magazine, introduced itself as "a forward-looking daring and wildly hedonistic magazine.... It will be the voice of the Turned-On Generation."

That "turned-on" generation, high school and college students, was going to Fenway by the thousands, filling the $2 bleacher seats, getting high on its first pennant race.

Sox fans, shivering and wrapped in blankets play a game of chess while they wait in line outside Fenway Park to buy tickets for the 1967 World Series.

Keith Richards, Brian Jones and Mick Jagger of the Rolling Stones are arrested on drug charges.

In a case of tragic misidentification, Israel downs USS Liberty in Mediterranean, killing 34 U.S. crewmen.

05.10.67   05.17.67   06.08.67   06.12.67

The Orioles and Red Sox play long ball with 10 home runs in a 12-8 Baltimore victory.

Supreme Court unanimously overturns laws that ban interracial marriages.

[CARL YASTRZEMSKI]

1967
Triple Crown Winner

THE YEAR OF YAZ

LEAGUE LEADER
BATTING AVERAGE • RBIs • HOME RUNS

Yastrzemski kicked into overdrive, on his way to a Triple Crown season of which the figures (.326, 44 homers, 121 RBIs) merely hint at his impact. The Red Sox won 16 of their final 27 games, a stretch in which Yaz went 40-for-96 (.417), driving in 26 runs and scoring 24.

BATTING AVERAGE		RUNS BATTED IN		HOME RUNS	
Yastrzemski, Bos	.326	Yastrzemski, Bos	121	Yastrzemski, Bos	44
F.Robinson, Bal	.311	F.Robinson, Bal	113	Killebrew, Min	44
Kaline, Det	.308	Killebrew, Min	94	Howard, Was	36
Scott, Bos	.303	Howard, Was	89	F.Robinson, Bal	30
Blair, Bal	.293	Oliva, Min	83		

RUNS		RUNS PRODUCED		DOUBLES	
Yastrzemski, Bos	112	Yastrzemski, Bos	189	Oliva, Min	34
Killebrew, Min	105	Killebrew, Min	174	Tovar, Min	32
Tovar, Min	98	F.Robinson, Bal	147	Yastrzemski, Bos	31
Kaline, Det	94	Kaline, Det	147	D.Johnson, Bal	30
McAuliffe, Det	92	B.Robinson, Bal	143	Campaneris, KC	29

BASE ON BALLS		ON BASE PERCENTAGE		SLUGGING AVERAGE	
Killebrew, Min	131	Yastrzemski, Bos	.421	Yastrzemski, Bos	.622
Mantle, NY	107	Kaline, Det	.415	F.Robinson, Bal	.576
McAuliffe, Det	105	Killebrew, Min	.413	Killebrew, Min	.558
Yastrzemski, Bos	91	F.Robinson, Bal	.408	Kaline, Det	.541
Kaline, Det	83	Mantle, NY	.394	Howard, Was	.511

HITS		TOTAL BASES		TOTAL PLAYER RATING	
Yastrzemski, Bos	189	Yastrzemski, Bos	360	Yastrzemski, Bos	7.3
Tovar, Min	173	Killebrew, Min	305	Kaline, Det	5.2
Scott, Bos	171	F.Robinson, Bal	276	B.Robinson, Bal	5.0
Fregosi, Cal	171	B.Robinson, Bal	265	F.Robinson, Bal	4.8
B.Robinson, Bal	164	Howard, Was	265	Blair, Bal	4.1

"THE IMPOSSIBLE DREAM"

Four teams — Boston, Minnesota, Chicago and Detroit — entered
the final week separated by 1½ games. It ended on the final
evening of the final day, with the Red Sox glued to a clubhouse
radio, listening as the California Angels eliminated the
Tigers in the second game of a doubleheader at Detroit.

On August 18, tragedy struck. Conigliaro was beaned by Angels righthander Jack Hamilton. The pitch busted up the left side of Conigliaro's face, damaged his vision and nearly killed him. Conigliaro's season-ending injury cost the Red Sox their cleanup hitter. O'Connell moved decisively, signing power hitter Ken "Hawk" Harrelson, a flamboyant and independent soul who, perhaps more than any major leaguer, personified the turbulent year.

Harrelson had been released by Kansas City Athletics owner Charlie Finley for, essentially, refusing to be subservient. Finley fined Harrelson for throwing baseballs to fans, wearing his socks the wrong way and assorted other acts of defiance. Finally, after Finley fined a teammate for drinking on a flight, Harrelson had had enough and blasted Finley in the newspapers, calling him a "menace" to baseball and "detrimental" to the game. Outraged, Finley released Harrelson. Thus Harrelson was a free agent (albeit a worried one) when O'Connell offered him a three-year contract and signing bonus worth $197,000. At the time Yastrzemski was the club's highest-paid player at $50,000; the total payroll was $825,000. Average major league salary in 1967 was $19,000; minimum was $6,000, only $1,000 more than in 1947.

The day Harrelson reported, his wardrobe of Nehru jackets in tow, two games separated the four contenders. On September 1, Harrelson had three hits and four RBIs in a 10-2 win over the White Sox. A standing-room crowd of 34,054 — Fenway sellouts now were commonplace — saw Jose Santiago pitch the Red Sox to a half-game lead over the Twins. On September 7 all four teams were tied for first place, separated by one percentage point.

Yastrzemski kicked into overdrive, on his way to a Triple Crown season of which the figures (.326, 44 homers, 121 RBIs) merely hint at his impact. The Red Sox won 16 of their final 27 games, a stretch in which Yaz went 40-for-96 (.417), drove in 26 runs and scored 24.

But nobody was folding. Minnesota rode the arms of Dean Chance and Jim Kaat and the bats of Harmon Killebrew, Tony Oliva and Rookie of the Year Rod Carew. Detroit's lineup included Al Kaline, Willie Horton and Bill Freehan, and a strong rotation with Mickey Lolich, Denny McLain and Earl Wilson (a former Red Sox pitcher on his way to a career-high 22 victories). The White Sox,

The Yankees' Thad Tillotson hits Joe Foy of the Red Sox in the head, and Jim Lonborg retaliates by hitting Tillotson. Tillotson then hits Lonborg. Next, Dick Howser is hit in the head by Lonborg. The benches emptied three times for fisticuffs.

06.21.67

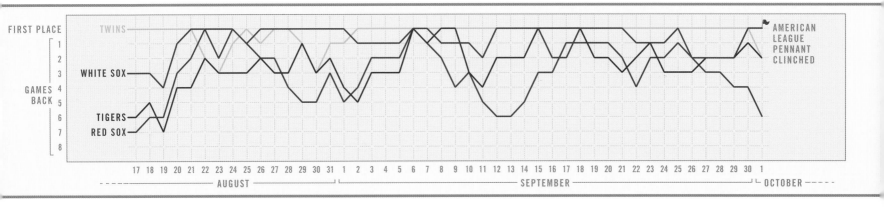

hitless wonders, did it with pitching: Starters Joel Horlen, Gary Peters, and Tommy John, and knuckleball relievers Wilbur Wood and Hoyt Wilhelm helped compile a 2.45 team ERA, the lowest since 1919.

On September 15, the Red Sox, Twins and Tigers were tied for first at 84-64, with the White Sox 1½ back at 83-66. On September 18 in Detroit, Yastrzemski's one-out shot into the upper deck tied the game in the ninth inning, and Dalton Jones won it, 6-5, with a home run off Mike Marshall in the 10th. The Red Sox beat the Tigers the next night, 4-2, with three runs in the ninth. Cardiac Kids, indeed. "For me, it was less pressure," Yastrzemski told writer Peter Gammons. "Before that, we'd have 8,000 people in the stands, and they all wanted to see a home run or a base hit. In 1967, if you made one good defensive play, they'd give you a standing ovation."

Entering the final week, the Twins had a half-game lead over the White Sox and a one-game lead over the Tigers and Red Sox. The schedule favored the White Sox, who had two games with the last-place Athletics and three games with the seventh-place Senators.

On Wednesday, September 27, the White Sox played a doubleheader in Kansas City while the Red Sox were off. Williams was desperate to hear the White Sox broadcast. "I took a six-pack of Miller beer and I climbed in the front seat of my car in the parking lot of my apartment building," Williams wrote. "There I sat through the evening and into the night, hoping and willing and wishing the White Sox to lose both games before I went nuts or my car battery died." The White Sox were swept by the A's, and two days later they were eliminated with a 1-0 loss to Washington.

One by one, the contenders unraveled. The Twins dropped two of three to the fifth-place Angels, while the Tigers split two games with the ninth-place Yankees. Meanwhile at Fenway, the Red Sox lost two to the eighth-place Indians — sending New England into a miserable funk.

On Saturday morning the Twins held a one-game lead over the Red Sox and Tigers. The Tigers, at home, faced back-to-back doubleheaders with the Angels, while the Twins arrived at Fenway for two.

"We would get to play the best to become the best — I couldn't wait," Williams wrote. "To me, it was almost like the World Series come early."

In the fourth inning at Fenway Park, Angels pitcher Jack Hamilton hits Tony Conigliaro in the face with a pitch, breaking his cheekbone and sending bone fragments into his eye. The 22-year-old Conigliaro is carried off the field and taken to Sancta Maria Hospital.

07.22.67   08.18.67

Nationally renowned poet and author Carl Sandburg dies at the age of 89.

Politicians and big-wigs elbowed for tickets. Minnesota Sen. Hubert Humphrey attended the weekend series as the guest of Massachusetts Sen. Edward Kennedy. On Saturday, Santiago pitched against Kaat, who pitched superbly until being forced to leave after suffering an elbow injury in the third inning. The Sox took a 2-1 lead in the fifth when reliever Jim Perry failed to cover first on a bad-hop grounder to the right side. Scott's 450-foot home run produced a 3-2 lead in the sixth.

Just before Scott connected, a station wagon knocked the rear bumper of a taxicab on Tremont Street at Boston Common. As reported in the Boston Herald Traveler, the "red-faced cigar-chewing" cabbie charged out of his vehicle and accosted the driver of the station wagon. But as the cabbie started to vent his spleen he overheard the radio inside the station wagon. "Scott hit a home run!" the cabbie shouted. Hostilities ceased.

The newspaper also reported the experience of a Red Line carman, Tom Kennedy, who was on duty but listening to his transistor radio during the game. Kennedy's radio lost reception when the subway car went underground. "We were ahead going into one tunnel and when we came up the score was tied," Kennedy complained. Passengers were glued to his radio. "One guy missed two stops," Kennedy said.

In the seventh, Yaz hammered a three-run homer, his 44th, inducing delirium. Killebrew answered with his 44th home run in the ninth, but the Sox held on for a 6-4 win. The unsung Santiago (12-4) allowed just two hits in seven innings. In Detroit, the Tigers split, leaving them a half-game back of the Red Sox and Twins.

Sunday was for everything, with Lonborg facing Chance, and the Tigers and Angels again playing two. Williams doubted the arm-weary Tigers could sweep; he thought the winner of the Red Sox-Twins game would own the pennant. Chance (20-13) had beaten the Sox four times that season, dominating them with a sharp sinker. Lonborg (21-9) was 0-6 lifetime against the Twins.

Chance dominated the first five innings and took a 2-0 lead into the bottom of the sixth. With Lonborg due to lead off, all eyes were on Williams. "Some thought I might send up a pinch-hitter for him," Williams wrote. "But he had become one of my toughest and smartest players, and if anyone could figure out a way to pull our ass out of the sling…" Lonborg bunted Chance's first pitch, surprising third baseman Cesar Tovar, and legged out a single. Singles by Adair and Jones loaded the bases for Yastrzemski, who — automatically — rapped a two-run single up the middle. A missed fielder's choice drove Chance from the mound, after which two wild pitches and an error put the Sox up, 5-2. That was all Lonborg needed.

Yaz cut short a Twins rally in the eighth by throwing out Bob Allison at second. When Petrocelli cradled a popup for the final out, fans surged onto the field and hoisted Lonborg, who happily bobbed upon a sea of shoulders. Long after the others, Lonborg appeared in the clubhouse, his uniform in tatters.

"It was great, then all of a sudden, it was terrifying," Lonborg told historian George Sullivan. "They were taking off my clothes. Somebody even took off my shoelace without taking off my shoe."

Champagne, however, remained on ice. The Tigers had won their first game, and if they won the second there would be a one-game playoff in Detroit the next day. But Denny McLain, on a sore ankle, could not hold a 3-1 lead and the Tigers trailed, 8-3, coming to bat in the bottom of the ninth. They cut the margin to 8-5 and put two runners on base with one out. With the Red Sox paralyzed in the clubhouse, and Williams listening in Yawkey's office, Dick McAuliffe rapped into a double play — ending the legendary pennant race.

Williams shouted, "It's over! It's over! It's over!" Yawkey, who hadn't touched liquor in years, raised a glass of champagne and toasted his belligerent manager. "I will drink to you," Yawkey said. Then he started to cry. Later, he embraced Yastrzemski and doubled his salary to $100,000 on the spot.

08.28.67

Red Sox take the first game against the Yankees, 2-1, in nine innings, Yanks win the second game in 20 innings, 4-3 — a doubleheader totaling eight hours, 19 minutes.

08.29.67

Ken "Hawk" Harrelson, released by Charles O. Finley for calling the Kansas City Athletics owner "detrimental to baseball" and refusing to retract the statement, is signed by the Red Sox.

"By the dawn's early light"
Young Red Sox fans sit atop a billboard at Fenway Park and await the start of the 1967 World Series.

WINS

22

[tied for first]

WIN PERCENTAGE

.710

[second]

COMPLETE GAMES

15

[second]

INNINGS PITCHED

273

[second]

BASE ON BALLS

83

"It was great, then all of a sudden, it was terrifying. They were taking off my clothes.
Somebody even took off my shoelace without taking off my shoe."

[**JIM LONBORG**] 1967 CY YOUNG AWARD WINNER

STRIKEOUTS

246

[first]

STRIKEOUTS/PER 9 INNINGS

8.10

[fourth]

EARNED RUN AVERAGE

3.16

SHUTOUTS

2

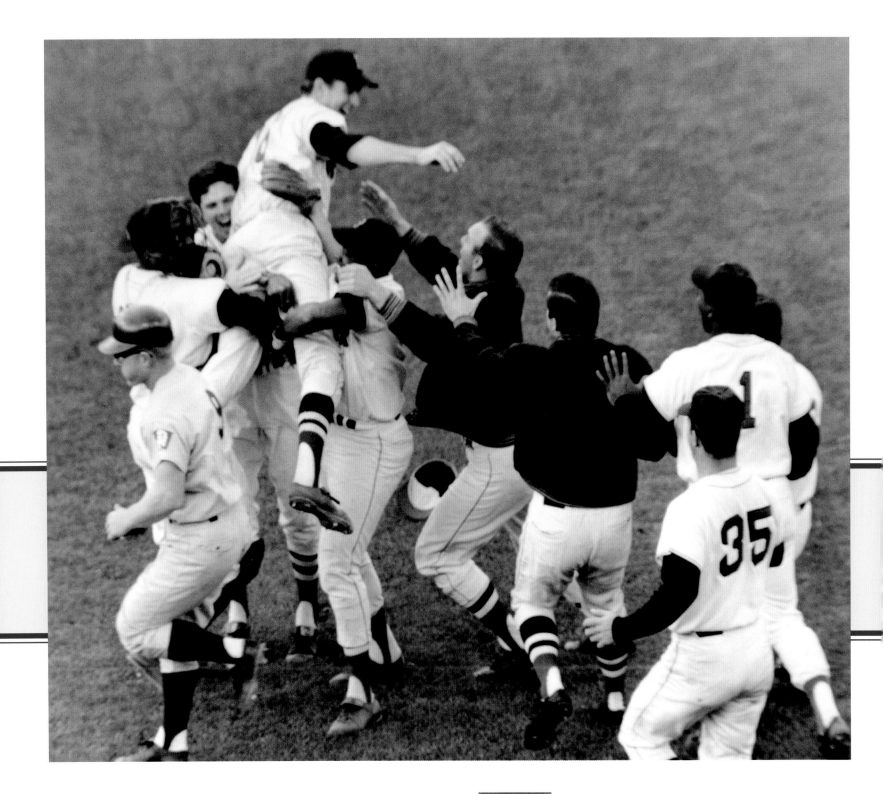

⚾ Jim Lonborg beats the visiting Twins, 5-3, in the final game
of the year, and the Angels beat the Tigers, 8-5, to give the
Red Sox the AL pennant — their first since 1946.

10.01.67   10.02.67

> Thurgood Marshall, nominated by President Lyndon B. Johnson,
is sworn in as the first black Supreme Court Justice.

The World Series was anticlimactic from New England's perspective. The heavily favored St. Louis Cardinals, winners of 101 games, were not swallowing the Impossible Dream. The Cardinals were fresh, and intimidating righthander Bob Gibson was at his Hall of Fame peak.

The Series belonged to Gibson. He pitched three complete games, struck out 26 and allowed just three runs. Lonborg countered with one-hit and three-hit gems. Yastrzemski hit .400, going 10-for-25 with three homers and five RBIs. In Game Seven at Fenway, Lonborg pitched on two days' rest and was hammered for 10 hits and seven runs. Williams left him in at least one inning too long-in a 7-2 loss. Gibson was overpowering. "I don't think we woke up to the fact that we were in the Series until we were halfway through it," Andrews says.

Losing the Series was but a minor disappointment to most. Yastrzemski was voted the American League MVP, and Lonborg won the AL Cy Young Award.

Williams was Manager of the Year, and O'Connell won the award for top executive. History remembers the 1967 Red Sox not as a great team, but as a great story.

They were a product of their moment in time, capturing the idealism and hubris of the 1960s, a we-can-change-the-world ethos scorning convention and established hierarchy. A 100-1 longshot winning the pennant? What next? An anti-war movement toppling a president? Gender equality? Environmental awareness? Racial tolerance? A man on the moon?

"It was such an exciting and chaotic time," Andrews says. "Everything was changing. Who can say? Maybe we fed into that as a team."

Petrocelli can't go a day without someone wanting to talk about the Impossible Dream. The strangers might have been 6 or 60 that season, but they all share the same sensation: "I remember it," they say, "like it was yesterday."

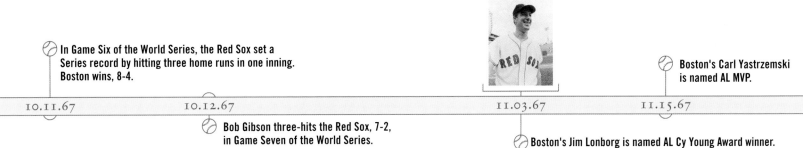

In Game Six of the World Series, the Red Sox set a
Series record by hitting three home runs in one inning.
Boston wins, 8-4.

Boston's Carl Yastrzemski
is named AL MVP.

10.11.67   10.12.67   11.03.67   11.15.67

Bob Gibson three-hits the Red Sox, 7-2,
in Game Seven of the World Series.

Boston's Jim Lonborg is named AL Cy Young Award winner.

The Rivalry

THE YANKEES AND THE RED SOX

6

BOSTON RED SOX VS. NEW YORK YANKEES

"Whenever the Red Sox prepared to play the Yankees, it was as if they were dressing up for battle. ... Against the Yankees we would button up differently, taking a little longer than usual to put on the uniform. We knew we were getting ready to take the field and uphold our values. It was as though we were knights in armor."

BILL LEE, *THE WRONG STUFF*

When it comes to just plain enmity, Athens and Sparta, the Capulets and the Montagues, the Hatfields and the McCoys don't have anything on the New York Yankees and Boston Red Sox. Haul out what verbs you will — hate, abhor, despise, detest — these are two teams that have it in for each other.

It starts before the first pitch. Like a Greek tragedy, every Yankees-Red Sox game is accompanied by a chorus, although it is not exactly what Euripides had in mind. "Yan-kees Suck!" wafts the echo from the cheap seats at Fenway Park. "Yan-kees Suck!" On a good day the animosity might manifest itself in the form of a Yankees cap plucked from the head of an interloper and ceremoniously placed in a urinal for the masses to defile. On a bad day, it's a hail of batteries aimed at the center fielder. (Don your batting helmet, Mickey Rivers.) To this day, the Yankees and their fans merit the chilliest New England welcome since the Boston Tea Party.

Of course, it's the other side of the coin when the Red Sox visit Yankee Stadium. Change the noun, keep the verb, chant the chant. "Bos-ton Sucks," bellow the bleacher bums — followed perhaps by a fight in the stands. For years, Yankees fans reveled in an even nastier chant, one that fully reflected the difference between the teams' fortunes. "Nine-teen Eight-een... Nine-teen Eight-een" — a reference to Boston's previous World Series championship before the Red Sox stunned the Yankees in

2004 by winning the final four games of the best-of-seven American League Championship Series and then swept the St. Louis Cardinals in the Series. When the Yankees and the Red Sox meet, it's more than a game. It's a clash of cultures, and neutrality is not allowed. As those Hatfields or McCoys might say: Either you're wit' us or a'gin' us.

The rivalry only begins — or perhaps ends — with baseball. Boston versus New York. It's the Old North Church versus the Statue of Liberty. The Museum of Fine Arts versus the Metropolitan Museum. Baked beans versus hot pastrami. Aerosmith versus the Ramones. The Boston Strangler versus Son of Sam. Nothing is sacred; nothing is off limits.

The Red Sox and the Yankees have engaged in memorable battles for more than a half century — the 1949 pennant race, the 1978 playoff game to decide the American League East champion, the 2003 and 2004 American League Championship Series — and hostilities between the clubs date back almost to their beginnings.

After the American League was formed in 1901, league president Ban Johnson forced the transfer of some of Boston's best players to New York in order to "level the playing field." Johnson's shuffling created ill will in Boston, and it certainly wasn't alleviated when the two teams battled for the pennant in 1904. The New York club, then known as the Highlanders, and the Boston club, then the Pilgrims, met in a season-ending series. Boston fans took a considerable

BAMBINO

How does a Red Sox fan define adding insult to injury? Flip through the team's record book and you find the name George Herman "Babe" Ruth all over it — as a pitcher. Although he pitched only five full seasons in Boston, the portly portsider is 17th in career wins with 89, ahead of Dennis Eckersley. Ruth is tied for 10th in career shutouts with 17, ahead of Lefty Grove. He's eighth in complete games (105), ahead of Roger Clemens. He's fourth in career ERA (2.19), just a tick behind leader Smoky Joe Wood (1.99). And he's second in winning percentage (.659), ahead of Cy Young.

Interestingly, Ruth's name doesn't appear among the Red Sox's season or career hitting leaders. One name from the deep, dark past does: Harry Hooper, a Hall of Fame outfielder, a key player on four Red Sox world championship teams between 1912 and 1918, who still holds the team's career record for triples with 160. However, Hooper's greatest contribution to baseball was suggesting that Ruth — who in various seasons led the American League in ERA, shutouts and complete games — move from the mound to the outfield.

RED SOX LEADERS: HITS PER 9 INNINGS

PLAYER	HITS PER 9/IP	INNINGS PITCHED
1) Pedro Martinez	6.79	1,384
2) **Babe Ruth**	**7.06**	1,190
3) Smokey Joe Wood	7.10	1,426
4) Carl Mays	7.48	1,105
5) Dutch Leonard	7.50	1,361

measure of satisfaction as the Pilgrims nosed out the Highlanders for the pennant. New York, though, had an answer. The National League champion New York Giants, and their legendary manager John McGraw, in a snoot over the upstart league, refused to play in the World Series, denying the Pilgrims a chance to repeat as world champions. Boston had beaten Pittsburgh in 1903 in the inaugural World Series.

Red Sox-Yankees hostilities escalated after a New Yorker, Harry Frazee, bought the Red Sox and proceeded to sell off the team's biggest stars, many to the Yankees, to finance his theatrical projects. The ultimate insult for Bostonians was Frazee selling Babe Ruth to the Yankees for $100,000 in 1920 to help finance the production of the play No No Nanette — a Broadway play, no less. The Red Sox, who had won five of the first 15 World Series, fell into a sea of mediocrity

to play, and two 20-game winners scheduled to pitch. The Sox took a 4-0 lead in the first game, but wound up losing twice, 5-4 and 5-3.

A rivalry demands at least a measure of equality between the combatants, and through the first three-quarters of the 20th century the Yankees and Red Sox largely competed at different levels. Between 1920 and 1970, the Yankees won 29 pennants, and the Sox finished within nine games of a pennant-winning Yankees team only once — the 1949 heartbreaker. In 1967, during Boston's "Impossible Dream" run to the World Series, the Yankees were mired deep in post-dynasty depression, finishing 20 games off the pace. As the Bicentennial approached, the playing field between the two teams had leveled out. The Baltimore Orioles dynasty was slipping, while the homegrown Red Sox and the hired-gun Yankees each fancied themselves as the AL East's heir apparent.

Babe Ruth poses with Yankees owner Colonel Jacob Ruppert after signing his first contract with the team.

while the Yankees became the most dominant team in sports.

The rivalry reached full boil in 1978, that classic season when the teams slugged it out toe to toe, shot for shot, Frazier and Ali on a baseball diamond, going the distance. For Red Sox fans, it was a season at once sacred and obscene, uplifting and heartbreaking, unforgettable and a source of collective amnesia. A season that encapsulated in 162 games — make that 163 — what it is to live and die with the Boys of Fenway.

This is not to dismiss the classic 1949 pennant race, when the Ted Williams-led Red Sox arrived at Yankee Stadium on the season's final weekend with a one-game lead over the Yankees with two games

How did hostilities begin? Call it a cultural thing, the natural friction between the haves and the have-nots. The Yankees traditionally were as blue chip as U.S. Steel, so spoiled by success that they would fire a manager for losing a World Series. The Red Sox were lovable losers with a Bohemian streak, their fans reveling not in box scores or standings but in the pastoral beauty of how-you-play-the-game.

"They were an elitist corporation with a self-promoted public image of cold arrogance that went against my grain," former Red Sox pitcher Bill Lee wrote of the Yankees in his autobiography *The Wrong Stuff*. "The Yankees represented the political right in baseball, while the Red Sox were their opposite number. We were composed of

New York's Thurman Munson (left) and Boston's George Scott (third, left) hold back the Yankees'
Bobby Murcer while Red Sox pitcher Ken Brett and umpire Merle Anthony restrain Red Sox catcher
Tom Satriano at Fenway Park, September 24, 1969. The fight started after Satriano tagged Murcer out.

the stuff that made this country great. We were like a bunch of modern-day pilgrims."

Ultimately the political becomes personal, and did things ever get personal. "In the 1970s it was bigger than what it is now," says Don Zimmer, who has been on both sides of the rivalry. "There were some players that disliked each other — that made it more intense as a rivalry. Graig Nettles and Bill Lee didn't get along. Carlton Fisk and Thurman Munson didn't get along — they were always at each other. It was kind of a war between the players."

How much did Munson loathe Fisk? One day he entered the clubhouse and saw mention in the Yankees' media notes that he was second in the league in assists among catchers — two behind Fisk. Munson sought out Yankees public relations director Marty Appel and read him the riot act. "What's the idea of showing me up like this?" Munson roared. "Do you think for one minute he has a better arm than me?" That night Munson dropped not one, not two, but

three third strikes. By making the easy pegs to first base for outs, he registered three assists and moved ahead of Fisk.

The first notable Red Sox-Yankees skirmish of that era came in mid-1973. After a collision at home plate, Fisk and Munson came up swinging. Gene Michael had missed a squeeze bunt attempt, and Fisk tagged out Munson at the plate.

Things got ugly on May 20, 1976 at Yankee Stadium, after Lou Piniella tried to take out Fisk at the plate. Fisk objected, and a brawl ensued. Lee, who was the Red Sox starter, was sucker-punched by Mickey Rivers and body-slammed Gorilla Monsoon-style by Nettles. "I guess Graig's idea of keeping the peace was to arrange for me to get a lot of bed rest in a quiet hospital," Lee said. When the injured Lee showered obscenities at Nettles, all hell broke loose again. "The entire scene became a Fellini movie," Lee said. "Forty-five thousand Yankees fans are screaming for the lions to devour the Christians." One fan ran on the field and attacked the injured Lee, who used his

10/1/1949 | NEW YORK

Ted Williams is a forlorn figure in a sea of jubilation as Yankees fans celebrate the home run by Johnny Lindell that broke a 4-4 tie and gave New York a 5-4 victory on the next-to-last day of the season. The win tied the Red Sox and Yankees for first place, and the Yankees won again a day later to capture the American League pennant.

spikes to defend himself. Lee suffered torn ligaments in his pitching shoulder and never was the same.

It all was a prelude to the 1978 season, one that Ron Shelton couldn't have scripted any tighter. Let's step back for a moment and meet the contestants.

Zimmer's Red Sox team was as full of promise as a phone call from Ed McMahon. Jim Rice and Fred Lynn seemed on the fast lane to Cooperstown, where they would reunite with Carl Yastrzemski every Induction Day. Dwight Evans was beginning to show the subtle combination of skills that made him arguably the most underrated player of his day. And for once things didn't turn into a Stephen King novel when the other team came up to the plate. The staff ace was Mike Torrez, who had won 14 games for the Yankees in 1977, plus two more in the World Series. Luis Tiant still was practicing modern dance on the mound, Dennis Eckersley was coming into his own during his first life as a starter, and Lee, firmly entrenched in Zimmer's doghouse — that's what you get for calling your manager names and losing seven straight starts — played clubhouse lawyer from the bullpen.

Their adversaries were one of the most disagreeable and dislikable teams in baseball history. Yankees manager Billy Martin hated his star slugger, Reggie Jackson. Reggie hated Billy. Munson hated everyone. The previous summer in Boston, Martin and Jackson almost came to blows after Jackson allowed a ball to drop in front of him in the outfield and Martin replaced him in mid-inning.

The Red Sox left the gate in 1978 like Secretariat, sprinting through the first half on a 111-win pace. "Boston won again and is 61 and 28, 14 games in front of us. Forget this season. The rest of the year is just playing out the string," wrote Sparky Lyle in *The Bronx Zoo*.

What happened? The Yankees got healthy, recovering from a series of injuries, and laid-back Bob Lemon replaced the fiery Martin. To the north, the Red Sox fell back to earth. Fisk, Lynn, Butch Hobson and Yastrzemski suffered injuries, and the team faltered. "It's all tied up in history, and that old Yankee fear," wrote Thomas Boswell, a columnist for the Washington Post. "Zimmer had little choice but to push his delicately balanced power plant until black smoke started pouring from the exhaust. Mythology forced his hand.

JIMMIE FOXX & LOU GEHRIG

Only a 20-game lead would suffice." Others put it more bluntly. "Some of these guys are choking," said Red Sox first baseman George Scott, who himself was wearing a 0-for-34 collar.

The details are ugly and, by now, familiar. The Red Sox entered September 6½ games ahead of the Yankees, but they lost six of eight prior to a four-game series with the Yankees in Boston. Martin, who had taken exception to Lee comparing him to Hermann Goering, paid a clubhouse boy to hang a dead mackerel in Lee's Fenway Park locker, along with a lewd suggestion of what he could do with it. It was worse on the field for the Sox — they lost all four games by a combined score of 42-9. ("Keeping score, I had begun to feel like an accountant for a Wall Street brokerage firm in the fall of 1929," wrote Roger Angell, a lifelong Red Sox fan, in the New Yorker.) The sweep came to be known as the Boston Massacre, a metaphor which no doubt set Paul Revere spinning in his grave. After losing two more at Yankee Stadium the following week, the Red Sox not only had squandered their 14-game lead but now were 3½ games in arrears.

But one part Rasputin, one part Rocky Balboa, the Red Sox would not die. They won their last eight games and 12 of their last 14. The Yankees clung to one-game lead until the season's final scheduled day. Toronto Blue Jays outfielder Sam Ewing sneaked into Fenway's scoreboard and put up an 8 for Cleveland, New York's opponent, setting the park abuzz. And improbably, life imitated artifice. The Indians hung a nine-spot on Catfish Hunter, the Fenway scoreboard paid tribute to the Cleveland starter ("Thank you, Rick Waits") and Luis Tiant beat Toronto, 5-0. Both the Yankees and the Red Sox had a 99-63 record. First one to 100 wins the AL East.

The one constant about baseball is that there always is tomorrow — except, as Yogi Berra might say, when there is no tomorrow. A one-game playoff for the pennant had happened only once previous in baseball history. And the Red Sox lost that one, 8-3, to the Cleveland Indians in 1948. This time the suffering in New England would be more exquisite.

If baseball is a game of inches, it never was more apparent than on that October afternoon. History dwells on the moment that

The Yankees' Reggie Jackson is greeted at home plate by Thurman Munson, Chris Chambliss and Mickey Rivers after belting a three-run home run at Fenway Park during the 1978 season.

Boston's 2-0 lead evaporated, when Bucky Dent, using a bat borrowed from Mickey Rivers, knocked an oh-so-unlikely, three-run tater over the Green Monster, silencing the Fenway Park faithful. "People were stunned," Dent says. "I could feel that eeriness: 'The black cat's here again.'" Torrez, who gave up the home run, remembers it another way: "Another half-inch in on his hands and I may have broken his bat."

Blame right fielder Piniella, too. In the sixth inning with two on, Lynn laced a liner to right field that looked good for extra bases. Piniella, never regarded as more than an adequate fielder, had sensed that pitcher Ron Guidry, a lefthander, was tiring. After consulting with Munson, Piniella shaded toward the line and was in position to snag Lynn's drive for an easy out. In the ninth, Pinella made one of the greatest plays ever that didn't result in an out. He lost Jerry Remy's drive in the late afternoon sun. But instead of panicking, Pinella bluffed, positioning himself as if he were about to make the catch. The ball bounced eight feet in front of Piniella.

Piniella's trickery kept Rick Burleson from reaching third base, where he might have scored and tied the game when Jim Rice flied to the outfield. If Reggie Jackson, an uncertain fielder, had been in right

field, the extended season might have stretched into extra innings. But as Yastrzemski observed, "If ifs and buts were candied nuts, we'd all have a helluva Christmas."

That October 2 afternoon was a microcosm of the season. The Red Sox jumped in front and padded their lead. The Yankees fought back, late, strong and improbably. The wounded Red Sox scratched and clawed, fighting back and falling short by the most miniscule of margins. A single run decided a season: Yankees 5, Red Sox 4.

Boswell dubbed it "The Greatest Game Ever Played." "For once baseball had achieved a moment of genuine dramatic art, a situation that needed no resolution to be perfect," he wrote. "A game, a season, and an entire athletic heritage for two cities had been brought to a razor's edge." Angell was less philosophical as he mused on the moment that Yaz's popup settled into Nettles' glove for the final out: "I think God was shelling a peanut."

The memories of 1978 live on. At his baseball camp, Dent constructed his own Little Fenway, with a scoreboard frozen forever at 3-2. When Zimmer joined the Yankees in 1983 as a coach, whose house did he rent? Dent's.

TED WILLIAMS AND JOE DiMAGGIO

The Clipper and The Splinter. Joe D and Teddy Ballgame. The 56-game hitting streak and the .406 season. Hemingway and Updike. For more than a half-century, Joe DiMaggio and Ted Williams have been mentioned in the same breath — even by their teams' general managers, who once discussed an even-up swap. Most baseball fans have tended to mention DiMaggio first, ranking him a little higher in the pantheon of baseball immortals. Is this fair? Let's take a look at the numbers.

CAREER NUMBERS

	YRS	G	BA	OBP	SLG	HR	RBI	R	BB	
WILLIAMS	19	2292	.344	.482	.634	521	1839	1798	2019	
DiMAGGIO	13	1736	.325	.398	.579	361	1537	1390	790	

The conclusion? DiMaggio certainly was a great hitter, but Williams arguably was the best ever to slap a pine-tar rag on a piece of ash. Williams has a big lead in virtually every significant offensive category. Pay special attention to his edge in walks, and the corresponding edge in on-base percentage, the most significant hitting statistic. Six times in his career, Williams posted an on-base percentage of .500 or higher, which meant that he reached base more often than he walked back to the dugout. DiMaggio didn't do it once. While both players were injury-prone and missed prime seasons because of military service, Williams had a significantly longer career than DiMaggio did. It is true that Fenway Park was a better hitter's park than Yankee Stadium, and Williams exploited it as well as any hitter ever has — his Beantown average was a stratospheric .361. Performance in road games narrows the gap between the two, but doesn't close it entirely.

CAREER NUMBERS ON THE ROAD

	G	BA	OBP	SLG	HR	RBI	R	
WILLIAMS	1127	.328	.468	.615	273	874	825	
DiMAGGIO	856	.333	.405	.610	213	817	740	

Any edge that fans give to DiMaggio seems built on intangibles. DiMaggio, by all accounts, was one of the great outfielders of all time. But Williams was better than his reputation indicates — his range factor (a measure of chances per game) is better than Lou Brock's and Carl Yastrzemski's. Baserunning? DiMaggio was great, but Williams was at least good. You can't dismiss DiMaggio's collection of championship rings — nine World Series titles in 13 years — but Williams didn't have nearly the supporting cast that DiMaggio did. Plug Williams' bat into the Yankees lineup, and it is reasonable to expect that the team would have had similar success. Unlike DiMaggio, Williams never was married to Marilyn Monroe and Paul Simon never wrote a song about him. But when it came to performing the hardest feat in sports — hitting a baseball — no one did it better than Ted Williams.

BOSTON
RED SOX

1973

NEW YORK
YANKEES

The Yankees-Red Sox rivalry moved on. Wade Boggs and Don Mattingly battled for the batting title to the final day of the 1986 season. Some dumb kid in the Bronx orchestrated his own little miracle by running onto the field as Mike Stanley was making the final out of a 1993 pennant-race game. The umpire called time, Stanley got another chance, and the Yanks won the game.

From 1998 to 2004, the Yankees won the AL East title every year, and the Red Sox always finished second. They first met in the league playoffs in 1999. Pedro Martinez endeared himself forever in Red Sox Nation by beating Roger Clemens, 13-1, in Game Three, but the Yankees won the series in five games, although two of the victories were tainted by missed umpire's calls.

Hostilities between the teams reached new heights in the 2003 AL Championship Series. The benches cleared twice in Game Three over beanball pitches. Zimmer charged after Martinez, who flipped the Yankees' 72-year-old coach to the ground. The Fenway Park atmosphere was so tense that beer sales were cut off in the fourth inning. In the ninth, Yankees pitcher Jeff Nelson and outfielder Karim Garcia got into a fight with a Boston groundskeeper in the bullpen and were charged with assault. The series came down to Game Seven at Yankee Stadium. The Red Sox took a 4-0 lead, but the Yankees tied the score, 5-5, against a tiring Martinez, who was left in the game by then-manager Grady Little, a decision that cost Little his job. The game droned into extra innings, and the Yankees won on Aaron Boone's home run in the 11th.

The teams were at it again in 2004. In a July game at Fenway, Red Sox catcher Jason Varitek shoved the Yankees' newest superstar, Alex

Yankees first baseman Tino Martinez reaches into the crowd to catch a foul ball off the bat of Boston's Jason Varitek in Game One of the 1999 AL Championship Series.

Rodriguez, in the face, and A-Rod wasn't about to take it. He swung back, and both benches emptied. Three months later, for the second straight year, the Red Sox and Yankees met for the American League pennant. The Yankees won the first three games and had a one-run lead in the ninth inning of Game Four with their great closer, Mariano Rivera, on the mound. But Boston tied the score and won in the 12th inning on David Ortiz's home run. Ortiz had another game-winning, walk-off hit a day later. Back at Yankee Stadium, gimpy-ankled Curt Schilling pitched brilliantly for the Red Sox in Game Six, and they won Game Seven in a rout, becoming the first team in major league history to overcome a 3-0 deficit.

And the chants echo on. As do the spirits of the combatants. In the spring of 2001, Bill Lee dredged up the 1978 pennant race like a grave robber, claiming in a radio interview that Zimmer, who is a close friend of Yankees owner George Steinbrenner, tanked the season. "The fix was in; it had to be," Lee taunted. "How could we cough up that big a lead? Only the Phillies and the Arabs lost in as quick a time."

Sure, Lee's notion was preposterous, even borderline delusional. But by its very existence, a conspiracy theory sends one message: It ain't over. The fact that a baseball game can inspire this level of paranoia speaks volumes about the vast differences between two teams, two constituencies, two cultures located just 200 miles apart.

The Title Years

THE RED SOX TEAMS OF 1903-1918

RED SOX TEAMS OF 1903-1918

"Boston clubs have never lost in a World Series and the championship deserves to remain here until the war is won."

RED SOX OWNER HARRY FRAZEE, 1918

Second baseman Dave Shean fielded a grounder and threw to Stuffy McInnis for the final out of the 1918 World Series. McInnis held the ball high and led a charge of Boston Red Sox players for the clubhouse. A brass band played "Tessie," a show tune that had become a Boston ballpark anthem. The Royal Rooters, an always-oiled and boisterous cheering throng of about 300, intercepted the players in front of the dugout and shook hands with their heroes.

It was September 11, 1918, 12 days after Ted Williams was born. The Red Sox were second in headlines to World War I, but second in baseball to none. Boston's superior pitching and defense — a lethal combination in baseball's "dead ball" era — had smothered the Chicago Cubs and delivered the franchise its third World Series title in four years. The Red Sox had won five of the first 15 World Series, two more than any other team.

The Red Sox of the early 1900s were a sparkling jewel on the bedazzling crown that was Boston, the cultural seat of the United States. By the mid-19th century, Boston's 60,000 residents included Daniel Webster and Ralph Waldo Emerson, Horace Mann and Henry Wadsworth Longfellow, Nathaniel Hawthorne and Oliver Wendell Holmes. "All I claim for Boston," Holmes said, "is that it is the thinking center of the continent, and therefore, of the planet." Boston was "The Hub," short for "The Hub of the Universe." Others called Boston the "new Athens," a worthy successor to the birth home of philosophy and science and the nurturer of mathematics and literature.

Exquisite architecture was commonplace in Boston. The Customs House, Faneuil Hall Marketplace, Hotel Vendome and Back Bay's Trinity Church graced the growing city, not to mention scores of elegant homes and mansions. Even New York newspapers urged its readers to "Hurry on!" and see the Bunker Hill Monument, already a world-famous shrine.

The Huntington Avenue Grounds was not among Boston's architectural achievements. The single-level, wooden structure served as the home of Boston's American League team (initially the Somersets, then the Pilgrims and finally the Red Sox) from 1901 to 1911 until Fenway Park was opened in 1912. The expansive and odd-shaped Huntington Avenue Grounds (440 feet to the left-field fence, 635 to center, 290 to right) was built on a wasteland of weeds and lumpy soil near the New Haven and Hartford Railroad tracks and had seats for 9,000.

Most patrons arrived at the ballpark on trolleys or trains. At the first World Series, in 1903, men — and very few women, noted the Boston Globe — filed into the Huntington Avenue Grounds wearing dark suits and bowler hats. The cheapest ticket cost 50 cents. Once the seats were filled, fans were placed beyond the outfielders, swelling attendance to about 11,500 for each of the first three games.

Boston's teams in the early 1900s included the likes of Tris Speaker, Duffy Lewis and Harry Hooper, all great hitters. But when summer turned to autumn, the Red Sox usually won because of the pitching of Cy Young, Bill Dinneen, Smoky Joe Wood, Ernie Shore, Dutch Leonard, Rube Foster and Carl Mays.

"Boston commands special attention as the town which was appointed by the destiny of nations to lead the civilization of North America."

RALPH WALDO EMERSON

And then there was George Herman Ruth, the Babe, who excelled both in the batter's box and on the mound. The Red Sox ranked first or second in the American League in team ERA nine times between 1903 and 1918. In 31 World Series games during that era, they won 13 games by one run and their opponents scored two runs or fewer in 17 games.

Players of that era often were at odds with team ownership and management over money. The players wanted to eliminate the reserve clause in their contracts that bound them to a club until the club disposed of them, a practice that limited a player's negotiating power. World Series financial shares often exceeded a player's annual income, which is why the Series games were so hotly contested.

The World Series quickly became the country's biggest sporting event. Newspapers covered the spectacle with painstaking thoroughness. The coverage largely was polite. "The best of order prevailed and both teams received liberal applause for good work," reported the Boston Globe after six errors were committed in the first World Series game, October 1, 1903.

The Red Sox won the first World Series and added four more titles in the succeeding 15 years. On the following pages is a look at each of Boston's championship years.

1903 WORLD SERIES

Boston Pilgrims vs. Pittsburgh Pirates

rowd control was an issue in Boston at the first World Series. Many fans climbed over the wooden fence at the Huntington Avenue Grounds when the police weren't looking, swelling attendance considerably beyond the listed capacity of 9,000. To accommodate everyone, officials allowed fans to stand on the field in foul territory and behind the outfielders.

The overflow crowds had a greater impact on the 1903 Series than any Series since. A ball hit into the crowd in Boston behind the outfielders was a ground-rule double. Reported the Boston Globe after Pittsburgh won the third game: "Four of the five two-base hits made by Pittsburgh were on weak flies into the crowd that the Boston outfielders could have taken behind their backs."

Boston fans displayed great exuberance for the Pilgrims — the team was renamed the Red Sox in 1907 — and none were more boisterous than the Royal Rooters, a raucous group fueled by drink and a passion for the home team. The ringleader of the Rooters was 'Nuf Ced

McGreevey, who got his nickname by ending lengthy disputes with a terse and final "'Nuf Ced." ("Freddy Parent is playing better shortstop than Honus Wagner in this Series. 'Nuf Ced.") The Rooters often broke into their rendition of the show tune "Tessie." When the great Honus Wagner of the Pirates fell into a slump during the Series, the Rooters chided him by changing the song's lyrics from "Tessie, I love you madly" to "Honus, why do you hit so badly?"

The Series was tied after six games. Game Seven was scheduled on a Friday in Pittsburgh, only to be postponed by Pirates owner Barney Dreyfuss, who cited cold weather. Dreyfuss' real motive was getting a bigger gate on Saturday and affording an extra day's rest for pitcher Deacon Phillippe, who had been working more frequently than normal.

The Saturday crowd at Exposition Park was 17,038, far more than there were seats; the overflow was directed to a roped-off area behind the outfielders. Of Boston's 11 hits off Phillippe, five were ground-rule triples into the crowd, several of which could have been caught easily on an unobstructed field. Boston won, 7-3, with Cy Young on the

286 WINS
170 LOSSES

1890—1900

WINS 225
LOSSES 146

1901—1911

511

CAREER WINS

CY YOUNG

316

CAREER LOSSES

mound. The Pilgrims then won the Series at home, 3-0, on Bill Dinneen's second shutout and third victory of the Series. Pittsburgh lost the final four games by a score of 31-8.

Boston players earned Series winner shares of $1,182 — less than the Pirates, who received shares of $1,316, thanks to Dreyfuss according his share of $6,669.56 to his players.

The Red Sox won the American League pennant again in 1904, but there was no World Series because the National League champion New York Giants refused to play. Giants owner John Brush and manager John McGraw had nothing but contempt for the upstart American League and its players who had defected from the National League.

TRIS SPEAKER

"the Grey Eagle"

1912

Batting Average

TY COBB, DETROIT	.409
JOE JACKSON, CLEVELAND	.395
TRIS SPEAKER, BOSTON	.383
NAP LAJOIE, CLEVELAND	.368
EDDIE COLLINS, PHILADELPHIA	.348

On Base Percentage

TRIS SPEAKER, BOSTON	.464
JOE JACKSON, CLEVELAND	.458
TY COBB, DETROIT	.456
EDDIE COLLINS, PHILADELPHIA	.450
NAP LAJOIE, CLEVELAND	.414

Runs

EDDIE COLLINS, PHILADELPHIA	137
TRIS SPEAKER, BOSTON	136
JOE JACKSON, CLEVELAND	121
TY COBB, DETROIT	120
HOME RUN BAKER, PHILADELPHIA	116

Doubles

TRIS SPEAKER, BOSTON	53
JOE JACKSON, CLEVELAND	44
HOME RUN BAKER, PHILADELPHIA	40
DUFFY LEWIS, BOSTON	36

Home Runs

TRIS SPEAKER, BOSTON	10
HOME RUN BAKER, PHILADELPHIA	10
TY COBB, DETROIT	7

1912
WORLD SERIES

Boston Red Sox vs. New York Giants

The World Series was gaining the momentum of an avalanche by 1912. In New York, more than 10,000 jockeyed two hours before game time for prime position to read the play-by-play flashed on an enormous electronic board on the façade of the Times Building in the south end of Times Square. President Taft listened to the Series via Navy wireless on his yacht off Newport, Rhode Island. (The wireless reports and Times Square electronic board reports were communications milestones.) Boston mayor John Fitzgerald, better known as "Honey Fitz," led a pilgrimage to New York, joining hundreds of Royal Rooters on four special trains. Upon arriving, the robust group marched from Grand Central Station up Broadway in a torchlight parade, with Fitzgerald exercising his tenor voice every few blocks. Giants manager John McGraw agreed to write a daily column during the Series for the New York Times. Scalpers sold tickets for $40 to $60 each, more than double what they fetched in the previous Series.

The Red Sox won 105 games in 1912. Their fortunes rode on the right arm of Smoky Joe Wood, who had a 34-5 record. Asked that year if he threw harder than Wood, Walter Johnson replied, "Mister, there's no man alive can throw harder than Joe Wood." The Giants finished with a 103-48 record, three .300 hitters and two 20-game winners, and they stole 319 bases, 67 more than any other team.

The Series was hardly an artistic success; the teams combined for 31 errors. It largely is remembered because the outcome turned on two balls that were not caught in the last half-inning of the final game.

The Series was tied at three games each when Wood took the mound in the seventh inning against Christy Mathewson in Fenway Park. The Giants broke a 1-1 tie in the 10th inning on hits by Fred Merkle and Red Murray. Mathewson needed only three outs, but he didn't get them. Clyde Engle lofted a fly ball to center field that hit Fred Snodgrass' glove and bounded away, enabling Engle to reach second base. After Snodgrass made an over-the-shoulder grab of Harry Hooper's drive, Mathewson walked weak-hitting Steve Yerkes. Tris Speaker lifted a foul pop between home and first base that clearly was first

THE BOSTON RED SOX 1912

baseman Merkle's play, but he pulled up when Mathewson called for catcher Chief Myers to catch it. Myers lunged and missed, extending the at-bat for Speaker, who laced a single that scored Engle and moved Yerkes to third. Duffy Lewis, batting .156 in the Series, was walked intentionally. Larry Gardner followed with a sacrifice fly that gave the Red Sox a 3-2 victory.

Boston players each drew a Series share of $4,024, greater than most of their salaries. Snodgrass' error became a part of baseball infamy. He became a wealthy banker and the mayor of Oxnard, California, but when he died in 1974 the headline on his obituary in the New York Times read: "Fred Snodgrass, 86, Dead, Ballplayer Muffed 1912 Fly".

FRED SNODGRASS - NEW YORK GIANTS

"For over half a century, I've had to live with the fact that I dropped a ball in the World Series."

CHAMPIONS 1912
RED SOX
WORLD'S SERIES
FENWAY PARK · BOSTON ·
Souvenir Biography and Score Book.

Price, 10 Cents

The Giants-Red Sox battle
was the best World Series to date.

It was not an artistic success; the teams combined for

31 errors.

It largely is remembered because the outcome turned on two balls
that were not caught in the last half-inning of the final game.

WORLD SERIES

Back-to-Back Championship Seasons

1915

BOSTON OVER PHILADELPHIA
in best-of-seven series, 4-1

1916

BOSTON OVER BROOKLYN
in best-of-seven series, 4-1

The Red Sox made short order of the Phillies, who had won only 90 games during the season. Although Fenway Park was just four years old, the Red Sox borrowed new Braves Field for their Series games from their National League brethren because it had a larger capacity than Fenway. Boston crowds of 42,300 and 41,096 generated more revenue for the players to divide, plus the distance from home plate to the left-field fence, 396 feet, helped contain the Phillies' power hitters.

Phillies outfielder Gavvy Cravath was the 1912 major league leader in home runs with 24, more than four other National League teams and 10 more than the Red Sox's total. Cravath benefited from the Phillies home park, the Baker Bowl, where the right center-field fence was 300 feet from home plate and the right-field fence was 272 feet away.

Rube Foster, Dutch Leonard and Ernie Shore pitched all 44 innings of the Series for Boston and limited the Phillies to 10 runs, a .182 batting average and one home run. The Red Sox didn't need their 20-year-old rookie lefthander, Babe Ruth, who had an 18-8 record during the season. Grover Cleveland Alexander, who would win 372 games during his career, pitched the Phillies to their only victory.

DUTCH LEONARD

The 1916 season started ominously for the Red Sox. They traded star centerfielder Tris Speaker to Cleveland for $50,000 on Opening Day after he resisted a cut in pay to $8,000. Boston had given Speaker an $18,000 salary two years earlier to keep him from jumping to the Federal League, which by 1916 had collapsed.

The Red Sox forged a 91-63 record on the arms of their top five pitchers, who combined for 89 wins. Rube Foster, Dutch Leonard and Ernie Shore, who had been the core of the staff, now had considerable help from Babe Ruth (23-12) and Carl Mays (19-13). The Boston pitchers held Brooklyn to a .200 average and eight runs in the final 40 innings of the Series. In Game 2, Ruth gave up an inside-the-park homer (actually a single that took a bad hop over center fielder Tilly Walker's head), then shut out Brooklyn for 13 innings as Boston won 2-1. Ruth's scoreless-innings streak in Series play would reach 29⅔ innings, a record that stood until 1961.

Red Sox infielder Jack Barry probably was the most fortunate player in baseball at the time. He had been on three of Connie Mack's Philadelphia Athletics teams that won the World Series. When Mack began a youth movement in the 1915 season and sold off most of his veteran players, Barry landed with the Red Sox and collected Series winner shares in 1915 and 1916. Although he never was a regular and never hit higher than .262, Barry earned significant additional income five times in a seven-year span.

1918
WORLD SERIES
Boston Red Sox vs. Chicago Cubs

Interest in baseball waned considerably in 1918. World War I was being waged in Europe, and several harsh winters had depleted the United States' coal supplies. Wheatless Mondays and Wednesdays and meatless Tuesdays were introduced by the U.S. government to help support U.S. troops abroad, and a conservation campaign of "heatless days," "lightless nights" and "gasless Sundays" was launched. Ballpark crowds fell by 17 percent in 1917 and another 41 percent in 1918. Over three years, major-league baseball attendance declined from 6.5 million to 3 million.

In May 1918, the provost marshal of the armed forces, General Enoch Crowder, announced a "work or fight" order, meant to force all men of draft age out of nonessential work and into the military or war-related work. When the war ended in November 1918, 247 major league players were serving in the military; three had been killed in action. The Red Sox played most of the 1918 season with only Harry Hooper and Everett Scott left from their everyday lineup of 1917. With a shortage of players, manager Ed Barrow made a bold move: Babe Ruth would play in the outfield or at first base on the days he didn't pitch.

The Red Sox, who won the American League pennant despite only 75 victories (the season was shortened by one month due to the war), were underdogs in the World Series. The Cubs had the top three winners in the National League: Hippo Vaughn (22), Claude Hendrix (20) and Lefty Tyler (19). Cubs manager Fred Mitchell used only lefthanders Vaughn and Tyler as starters in the Series because it was Boston's practice to deploy the left-handed-hitting Ruth only against right-handed pitching.

Mitchell's strategy worked. Keeping Ruth on the bench helped the Cubs forge a 1.04 ERA, a Series record. Chicago yielded only six earned runs in six games, but the Cubs were undone by three unearned runs. Boston's victories were by scores of 1-0, 2-1, 3-2 and 2-1. The Red Sox scored just nine runs and batted only .186. Neither team hit a home run, the only homer-less Series ever.

The start of Game 5 was delayed for more than an hour while the players sought a guarantee that they would be paid shares of $2,000 (winning side) and $1,400 (losing side), per an earlier agreement. However, the agreement was based on gate receipts of $150,000 through four games, and the receipts were $128,755 at that point. After considerable arm-twisting by baseball officials, the players agreed to proceed with the Series. Boston mayor John Fitzgerald walked onto the field at Fenway Park and announced that although the players thought they were being wronged, they "have agreed to play for the sake of the public and the wounded soldiers in the stands." The public, however, was put off; the crowd for Game 6 was 15,238, some 9,000 less than for Game 5. The Red Sox's Series share was $1,102; the Cubs' was $671 — record lows.

The Red Sox would not return to the World Series until 1946. After the team slipped to sixth place in 1919, club owner Harry Frazee began discarding players. In January 1920, he sold Babe Ruth to the New York Yankees to help finance a Broadway play he was backing. It would be more than a decade before the Red Sox again ended a season with a winning record.

HARRY HOOPER

The Unforgettables

TED'S 1941 SEASON-ENDING DOUBLEHEADER; MEMORABLE MOMENTS AND CHARACTERS

by Steve Buckley, Jerry Crasnick and David Scott

1941

TED WILLIAMS

TED'S 1941 SEASON-ENDING DOUBLEHEADER

It is undoubtedly the most famous downtown stroll in baseball history, a lazy, weekend ramble whose destination was nowhere and everywhere. While Ted Williams carried no bags as he wandered the streets of Philadelphia on that September Saturday night in 1941, the walk must have been exhausting. He was, after all, carrying the weight of the world on his slender shoulders.

Williams was just 23 years old. The Kid really was a kid. Yet he was kneeling in the on-deck circle of baseball history. With two games remaining in the 1941 season — a Sunday afternoon doubleheader with the Philadelphia Athletics at Shibe Park — Williams had in his sights the specter of being the game's first .400 hitter since the New York Giants' Bill Terry hit .401 in 1930.

The story goes that the night before the doubleheader, after going 1 for 4 in that day's game to drop his average to .39955, Williams toured downtown Philadelphia with Red Sox clubhouse attendant Johnny Orlando — and did a lot of thinking about this .400 business while on the extended walk. The story continues that Orlando popped into a bar or two along the way, and that Williams, ever the all-American boy, tossed down a couple of malteds.

The next day, Teddy Ballgame belted shots all over Shibe Park, amassing six hits in eight at-bats in the doubleheader. When the day and the season and the quest were over, Williams was the owner of a .406 batting average. As sports writer Jack Malaney put it so well in the next day's Boston Post: "All hail Thumping Theodore Samuel Williams, the greatest batsman in a decade and one of the greatest of any time, because of his deeds during the 1941 season."

Deeds...indeed. But if Williams really knew how big a deal the season-ending doubleheader with the Athletics was going to be,

chances are he might have reached for something a tad more stiff than a malted. Pressure? What Williams did not know that day, couldn't possibly have known, is that his .406 season would turn out to be a dividing line in baseball history. For in all the seasons that have been logged since 1941, of all the hopeful maybes who have dug in against imposing pitchers and even more imposing history, and attempted to match or eclipse Williams, nobody has come close.

When Rod Carew flirted with .400 in 1977, it was such a big deal that it made the cover of Time magazine. Carew settled in at an impressive, but not historic, .388. Three years later, George Brett's bid ended at .390. The best Tony Gwynn did was .394 — in the ballpark with Williams, if you will, but an abbreviated quest because of the players' strike that ended the 1994 season. Wade Boggs, the Red Sox's best hitter for average since Williams, once hit .368. A great season, yet without a hint of 1941 to it.

Come next season, the game's top batsmen again will be dreaming — daydreaming, really — of becoming baseball's first .400 hitter in more than six decades. In 1941, Williams was hoping to become baseball's first .400 hitter in a little more than one decade. "The 1941 season really was the end of an era," says Dominic DiMaggio, Williams' Red Sox teammate and kid brother of the great Joe DiMaggio. "It was the last season before World War II. After the war, Jackie Robinson broke the color barrier. And later on we had

What Williams did not know that day, couldn't possibly have known, is that his .406 season would turn out to be a dividing line in baseball history. For in all the seasons that have been logged since 1941, of all the hopeful maybes who have dug in against imposing pitchers, and even more imposing history, and attempted to match or eclipse Williams, nobody has come close.

television, expansion, teams moving, all kinds of things. So you look closely at 1941 and you realize how special it was. It was a fabulous year in all respects, and we didn't even know it at the time."

The dominant baseball story of the 1941 season was Joe DiMaggio's 56-game hitting streak. It was an ever-building, ever-widening story that captured the imagination of millions of Americans — whether they were ball fans or not — and when it ended on July 17, 1941, it was shocking, stop-the-press news. It didn't hurt DiMaggio any that he was a more glamorous player than Williams, doing business with a more glamorous team, playing in a

town whose top athletes palled around with chorus girls, mobsters and Runyonesque barkeeps. Thus, as the season was winding down and Williams was making his bid for .400, the Story of the Year already had been written and filed: DiMaggio's hitting streak.

When Williams achieved his goal, he didn't have a horde of nationally known sports writers weighing in from Shibe Park; it wasn't even the lead story of the day. Most newspapers seemed more interested in the Joe Louis-Lou Nova heavyweight boxing showdown scheduled for the following night in New York at the Polo Grounds. (To understand the magnitude of a heavyweight title fight in those

The dominant baseball story of the 1941 season was Joe DiMaggio's 56-game hitting streak. It was an ever-building, ever-widening story that captured the imagination of millions of Americans — whether they were ball fans or not — and when it ended on July 17, 1941, it was shocking, stop-the-press news.

days, consider this: a mob of 56,549 fight fans turned out at the Polo Grounds to watch Louis KO Nova in the sixth round. A day earlier in Philadelphia, 10,268 showed up at Shibe Park to watch Williams make history. More than 60 years later, we still are waxing about Ted's .406 batting average, whereas the Louis-Nova fight is an obscure line in boxing almanacs.)

Williams didn't even have the spotlight to himself in the Boston newspapers. The sports editors of the day saved the biggest and boldest headlines for the Boston

College-Tulane football game played in New Orleans that Saturday. Boston's best-known sports columnist of the time, the Daily Record's Dave Egan, a man who later would become Williams' longtime nemesis, managed to take in both the BC-Tulane game in New Orleans and the Louis-Nova fight in New York — but he didn't have room on his itinerary for Ted's quest for .400.

It's not as if the possibility of Williams hitting .400 sneaked up on everybody. The Kid was a smash hit when he broke into the big

leagues in 1939, hitting .327 with 31 home runs and a league-leading 145 RBIs. The next season, Williams hit .344. When the 1941 season opened, Williams immediately made his case: He hit an Opening Day home run in Detroit, followed by a home run at Chicago's Comiskey Park that was said to travel some 500 feet. He had arrived late for spring training and been hampered by an ankle injury, but the season in bloom, the games being played for real, Williams swung with a vengeance. He hit .557 during a 16-game stretch in May, and at one point his average was .438.

EVEN THE GREATEST HITTERS EXIST IN THE SHADOW OF TED WILLIAMS. DESPITE LEADING THE LEAGUE IN WALKS EIGHT TIMES AND MISSING VIRTUALLY FIVE ENTIRE SEASONS TO MILITARY SERVICE, THE "SPLENDID SPLINTER" REMAINS THE MODEL TO

TED WILLIAMS' STRIKE ZONE

WHICH ALL OTHERS ARE COMPARED. THE CHART IS AN ENLARGED VERSION OF WILLIAMS' STRIKE ZONE. THE NUMBER ON EACH BALL REPRESENTS WILLIAMS' LIKELY BATTING AVERAGE IF EVERY PITCH CROSSED THE PLATE AT THAT LOCATION.

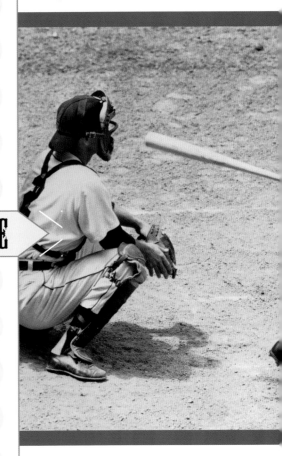

When the American League and National League convened for the All-Star Game, Williams was hitting .405 and DiMaggio's hitting streak stood at 48 games. The Red Sox opened the second half of the season in Detroit, and, ominously, Williams suffered another ankle injury. He spent the next two weeks on the bench, mostly watching, occasionally pinch-hitting, and his average dipped to .393.

The Red Sox played their final home game of the 1941 season on Sunday, September 21, after which the team traveled to

Washington and Philadelphia for the final six games of the schedule. Williams was at .406 when the trip began; after getting only two hits in 10 at-bats against the Senators, he was down to .402.

Though the Red Sox were well out of the pennant race by September — they finished in second place, 17 games behind the Yankees — Williams' quest for a .400 season kept the team in the headlines. Things even turned controversial: When Williams was called safe at first in the fourth inning of the September 24 game at Washington, some

something to get his mind off the great quest, for it was clearly an obsession at this point. Pitcher Charlie Wagner, Williams' roommate on the 1941 Red Sox, recalled 60 years later: "Those last few days of the season, it's all he thought about. Ted always got up early in the morning, but that weekend in Philadelphia he was up even earlier than usual. I remember that Saturday morning, the day before the season ended, I was still in bed and I could hear him shaving in the bathroom. He didn't talk much about it, but you knew it was on his mind."

.300	.320	.320	.330	.330	.315	.310
.310	.340	.340	.350	.340	.340	.320
.310	.310	.340	.350	.340	.340	.320
.340	.380	.380	.400	.390	.390	.320
.360	.390	.390	.400	.390	.390	.320
.360	.390	.390	.400	.380	.380	.310
.320	.340	.340	.330	.300	.300	.280
.320	.340	.330	.330	.275	.270	.260
.280	.300	.300	.300	.260	.250	.250
.270	.290	.300	.300	.250	.240	.240
.250	.270	.270	.260	.240	.240	.230

argued that the fix was in. The Boston Herald reported that many of the 7,500 fans at Griffith Stadium "hooted loud and long" when umpire Bill Grieve ruled that Ted had beaten out the grounder.

The Red Sox next traveled to Philadelphia to close the season against Connie Mack's Athletics. Friday was an off-day, and Williams went to Shibe Park with Red Sox coaches Frank Shellenback and Tom Daly and backup infielder Scoops Carey for an afternoon of batting practice. No doubt Williams wanted to get out of his room and do

If Williams feared anything it was that Mack, the 79-year-old owner/manager of the Athletics, would not allow his pitchers to throw anything "good" to Williams. It was a ploy that Mack often had used against Williams. The logic was simple: Why allow a team's best player to beat you? But the word was that Mack was going to give Williams a sporting chance to hit .400. Bert Whitman wrote in the Saturday, September 27 *Boston Herald*: "We understand the A's pitchers will pitch to him, will dare him to hit their best stuff, properly delivered. This is the

sporting thing to do, and the A's front office realizes that the crowd wants to see Ted hit, and not walk." Al Brancato, a 22-year-old infielder on the 1941 Athletics, recalled a clubhouse meeting before the series in which Mack "…Stood right in the middle of the room and made it quite clear to us that we were going to pitch to Ted Williams. He wanted Ted to earn it, which means we weren't going to give him anything to hit, but that we weren't going to walk him, either."

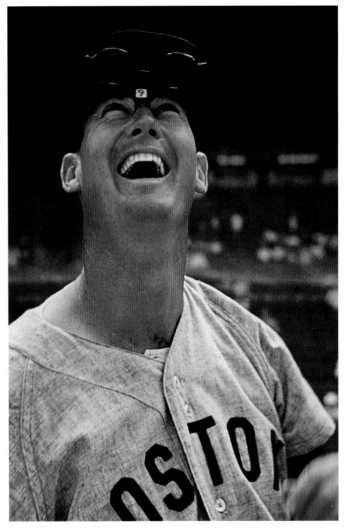

Only about 1,000 fans showed up at Shibe Park that afternoon. Mack's pitching rotation for the series was three rookies, the first a 30-year-old knuckleball artist named Roger Wolff who was making just his second big league start. (Finding a home with the Washington Senators in 1945, Wolff would win 20 games.) Williams drew a walk his first time up. In his next at-bat, he doubled to right-center to improve his average to .402. In his next two tries, he flied to right and hit a foul pop to first. With two outs in the ninth, he waved at a knuckleball for strike three. He went 1-for-4 in the Red Sox's 5-1 victory, dropping his average to .39955.

There has been a lot of revised, tinkered history over the years claiming that Williams, had he sat out the season-ending doubleheader, still would have had his .400 season, since the .39955 would have been rounded up to .400. Not so. If you don't hit .400, you don't hit .400, and no amount of mathematical wizardry was going to turn .39955 into .400. Wrote Bert Whitman in the September 28 Herald: "If it rains (Sunday) and washes out the last day of the season doubleheader between the Red Sox and A's, a

just 20 years old, and had spent most of the season in the minors. This historic game would be just his fourth major league appearance, which means Williams didn't know much about him. But the opposing players sure knew about Ted. Wrote Williams in his autobiography, *My Turn At Bat*:

"As I came to bat for the first time that day, the Philadelphia catcher, Frankie Hayes, said, 'Ted, Mr. Mack told us if we let up on you he'll run us out of baseball. I wish you all the luck in the world, but we're not giving you a damn thing.' Bill McGowan was the plate umpire, and I'll never forget it. Just as I stepped in, he called

"There was no way he was going to miss that last day," said Dom DiMaggio. "If anything, there might have been talk he'd sit out the second game if he had enough hits in the first game to hit .400. But he was going to play in that first game." Added Charlie Wagner, "I don't remember him saying anything about not playing. I don't think he ever considered it."

tremendous controversy might start as to whether Ted Williams, the Hub's Splendid Splinter, is entitled to be listed among the immortal .400 hitters in the majors."

"There was no way he was going to miss that last day," Dom DiMaggio said. "If anything, there might have been talk he'd sit out the second game if he had enough hits in the first game to hit .400. But he was going to play in that first game." Added Charlie Wagner, "I don't remember him saying anything about not playing. I don't think he ever considered it."

Starting for Philadelphia in the Sunday opener was righthander Dick Fowler. Unlike the knuckleballing Wolff, this rookie was a kid,

time and slowly walked around the plate, bent over and began dusting it off. Without looking up, he said, 'To hit .400 a batter has got to be loose. He has got to be loose.' I guess I couldn't have been much looser."

Williams got ahead on the count 2-and-0. Fowler threw a fastball, and Williams lined it to the right of first baseman Bob Johnson for a single. "That's the one I remember the most," Al Brancato said. "Our regular first baseman was Dick Siebert, but he was out and had gone home for the season. Bob Johnson usually played the outfield. That ball that went by him was hit so hard that you kind of knew the way the day was going to go."

And so it went. In his next at-bat Williams hit his 37th home run of the season, a shot that traveled over the right-field wall at Shibe Park and out onto 20th Street. Newspaper accounts estimated the distance at 440 feet.

When Williams came to bat in the sixth inning, lefty Porter Vaughan was pitching. Ted singled. In the seventh inning, facing Vaughan again, he hit a liner over Johnson's head for his fourth hit of the game, raising his average to .405. In his fifth at-bat, in the ninth, he hit a hard grounder to second baseman Crash Davis (yes, that Crash Davis) that was bobbled — an error — and Williams ended the game 4-for-5.

Williams now was hitting .404. He could have sat out the second game and nobody would have been able to wage an argument that his .400 season was tainted. Even if he had gone 0-for-4, his season-ending average would have been .4004376. Williams played — and continued to hit.

Mack's choice to pitch the second game was 22-year-old Fred Caligiuri. A "pretty slick righthander," according to one newspaper account, Caligiuri had spent most of the season with the Wilmington Blue Rocks in the Class B Interstate League, and had been the league's pitcher of the year. His season-ending start for the A's was just his fifth such big league assignment.

Facing Caligiuri in the second inning, Williams reached on a ground-ball single between first and second. In the fourth inning, he fouled off a 2-and-0 pitch and then hammered a fastball to right-center for a double. "The ball plunked into the loudspeaker horns on the wall, high up, punched a clean hole in one of them, and fell back on the playing field, just a two-bagger...but a tremendous clout just the same," reported the Boston Herald.

By the time Williams came to bat in the seventh inning, the sky was darkening and sports writers were filing their celebratory prose.

Williams flied to left, and his magical season was in the books: .4057. There being no controversy with the math this time, it was rounded off to .406.

Overshadowed by Williams' performance in the second game was the curtain-call performance of Lefty Grove, making his final big league start. Grove had had his greatest years in Shibe Park, pitching for Mack's Athletics, but now he was sweating out his eighth, and final, season with the Red Sox. The 41-year-old was torched for three runs in the first inning, prompting the Herald's Whitman to refer to him as "...That pathetic figure." But what praise the knights of the keyboard heaped upon Williams.

"Ted Williams put on one of the most spectacular last-day batting splurges in the history of major league baseball," wrote an enthusiastic Whitman. Fred Wright of the Boston Traveler could barely contain himself: "Ted did it! That, in three words, is a summarization of Boston's major league baseball for 1941." Gushed the Boston Globe: "Four hundred and six, or .4057 if you want to split decimal points. That's the fabulous figure with which Ted Williams finished the American League season today, as he became the first major league hitter to reach .400 in 11 years...by unleashing a hat-hoisting garrison finish."

Yet all they knew then was that Williams had become baseball's first .400 hitter since 1930, that he was the first American Leaguer to do it since the Detroit Tigers' Harry Heilmann hit .403 in 1923, that he was the first Boston player to do it since Hughie Duffy's .438 season with the 1894 Beaneaters.

Williams didn't just close out a season when he hit .406, he closed out a distinct chapter in baseball history. More than 60 years later, the game's best and brightest hitters still are trying to recapture the magic of that September Sunday afternoon at Shibe Park.

THE GREAT TED WILLIAMS

1939   1960

BATTING AVG.

1939 » .327	1952 » .400*
1940 » .344	1953 » .407*
1941 » .406	1954 » .345*
1942 » .356	1955 » .356*
1946 » .342	1956 » .345
1947 » .343	1957 » .388
1948 » .369	1958 » .328
1949 » .343	1959 » .254*
1950 » .317*	1960 » .316*
1951 » .318	CAREER » .344

* NOT ENOUGH AT-BATS TO QUALIFY FOR THE BATTING TITLE

TED'S LAST HOME RUN

SEPTEMBER 28, 1960

THOSE FANS, HOWEVER SPARSE AND BONE-CHILLED, WERE PART OF THE GLORIOUS MOMENT WHEN IN HIS FINAL AT BAT, WILLIAMS LAUNCHED A 1-1 PITCH FROM JACK FISHER INTO THE RED SOX BULLPEN. EVEN AS BEDLAM ENSUED AT THE OLD BALLYARD, THE 42-YEAR-OLD WILLIAMS, EVER THE STATESMAN, SHOWED LITTLE EMOTION AS HE QUICKLY CIRCLED THE BASES WITH HIS HEAD DOWN, HUMBLY.

TED'S FINAL AT-BAT

There are exits, there are graceful exits, and then there is the Ted Williams exit, which came on a cool, gray day with Fenway filled only to about a third of capacity. Earlier in the week, Red Sox owner Tom Yawkey had announced that Williams would be retiring, but many in Boston questioned the legitimacy of the retirement. With Baltimore in town for the Sox's final two home games, Williams was honored briefly by Boston mayor John Collins. Teddy Ballgame, after taking one last swipe at the "Knights of the Keyboard" and the "disagreeable things that have been said about me," conceded that "baseball has been the most wonderful thing in my life." He concluded his brief remarks by saying he couldn't think of a better place to spend his 19-year career than Boston, "with the greatest owner in baseball and the greatest fans in America."

Those fans, however sparse and bone-chilled, were part of the glorious moment when in his final at-bat, Williams launched a 1-1 pitch from Jack Fisher into the Red Sox bullpen. Even as bedlam ensued at the old ballyard, the 42-year-old Williams, ever the statesman, showed little emotion as he quickly circled the bases with his head down, humbly. The Sox finished the season in New York, but Williams had decided he would end his career in his park. The 521st and final home run of Williams' career came in the House that Ted Built.

1975 WORLD SERIES, GAME SIX

OCTOBER 21, 1975

THE VIDEO FROM AN NBC CAMERA IS AS MUCH A PART OF BASEBALL AS BABE,
CAL AND THE McGWIRE/SOSA HOME-RUN CHASE. BUT THE STRANGE THING
ABOUT CARLTON FISK'S "IF IT STAYS FAIR IT'S GONE" GAME-WINNING HOME RUN IN
GAME SIX OF THE 1975 WORLD SERIES, IS THAT IT WAS JUST ONE OF BOSTON'S
MIRACLE MOMENTS FROM THE 12-INNING EPIC BATTLE WITH THE CINCINNATI REDS.

DWIGHT EVANS' CATCH   BERNIE CARBO'S HOME RUN   CARLTON FISK'S HOME RUN

After three rain-induced postponements, the game finally began on Tuesday, October 21, at Fenway Park. The Red Sox, who trailed 3-games-to-2 in the series, took an early 3-0 lead. But the Big Red Machine was leading, 6-3, heading into the home half of the eighth inning.

With two on and two outs, Red Sox manager Darrell Johnson called on Bernie Carbo to pinch hit again. (Carbo previously had cracked a pinch-hit homer in the Series.) Carbo barely fouled off a 2-2 pitch from reliever Rawley Eastwick, then sent the next offering into the center field bleachers, and Fenway shook to its core as the Sox tied the score, 6-6.

The score was still tied in the 11th inning, and with a man on base, Cincinnati's Joe Morgan sent a deep shot to right that seemed destined to leave the yard and give the Reds a two-run lead. Just as heads began to hang in disbelief throughout Fenway, Dwight Evans made a spectacular grab to the right of the outfield bullpens, then spun and threw a bullet toward the infield that started an inning-ending double play.

That helped set the stage for Fisk's heroics in the 12th, memorialized by Dick Stockton's oft-heard call of the shot: "He swings, long drive to left field. If it stays fair it's gone...HOME RUN! The Red Sox win and the Series is tied." Without question, Miracle Three of the evening had been accomplished.

Smoky Joe Wood's Best Season

34*-5	.872*	38	35*	10*	344	258	1.91
* LEAD THE LEAGUE W-L	PCT.	GS	CG	SHUTOUTS	IP	SO	ERA

JOE WOOD VS WALTER JOHNSON

SEPTEMBER 6, 1912

WALTER JOHNSON, THE BIG TRAIN, WAS THE LEGENDARY WASHINGTON SENATORS FIREBALLER; SMOKY JOE WOOD WAS THE NEW KID ON THE BLOCK.

SMOKY JOE WOOD

WALTER JOHNSON

If this matchup had been played out in the modern era of televised sports, it well could have been the most-watched baseball event of all-time. Instead, it was played in 1912, when Fenway Park was brand new. Walter Johnson, the Big Train, was the legendary Washington Senators fireballer; Smoky Joe Wood was the new kid on the block. Earlier that season Johnson won 16 straight games, and Wood was working on a 13-game streak. Baseball's two most dominant pitchers were not scheduled to face each other during the series, but the Senators boldly challenged the Red Sox to pit Wood against Johnson; Senators manager Clark Griffith went so far as to say Wood would be "a coward" not to face Johnson. The challenge was accepted, and Fenway overflowed with fans for the game. For the first and only time in the history of Fenway Park, fans who didn't have a seat were allowed to stand along both foul lines and behind home plate, forcing the players to come out of the dugout in order to see the duel.

The game lived up to all the hype. Wood beat Johnson, 1-0. The Sox scored the only run with two outs in the sixth when Tris Speaker and Duffy Lewis hit back-to-back doubles. Wood won his 14th straight game by yielding six hits and fanning nine. Johnson gave up five hits and struck out five. Wood went on to win 34 games that season.

1999 ALL-STAR GAME

JULY 13, 1999

WHEN THE GAME STARTED, PEDRO MARTINEZ PITCHED HIMSELF INTO THE ALL-STAR GAME RECORD BOOK BY STRIKING OUT THE FIRST FOUR HITTERS AND FIVE OVERALL. "I THINK IT MAKES IT A LITTLE MORE SPECIAL, BEING HERE IN BOSTON," MARTINEZ SAID AFTER WINNING THE GAME'S MVP AWARD.

TED WILLIAMS WITH TONY GWYNN

If there is a better sports town in America than Boston it better start proving it, because Beantown has held top honors since the days of Russell, Orr and Ted. Even when the teams are losing, the talk is heated and passionate; the support solid and enduring. All that bragging aside, Boston proved it again when the 1999 All-Star Game festivities were played out at Fenway Park. In addition to the normal buzz that alone would surround the event, Major League Baseball wrapped in its All-Century team celebration for good measure. All the planned events seemed to fall short of what it meant to have hometown heroes Pedro Martinez and Nomar Garciaparra playing feature roles for the American League. The dramatic entry of living members of the All-Century team set the tone for the impromptu, emotional show of respect for Boston's best ever,

Ted Williams, whose introduction stirred a fever-pitched crowd. Mark McGwire, Sammy Sosa, Tony Gwynn, Ken Griffey, Jr. and other greats of past and present encircled and honored the living legend Williams. For pure goosebumps-and-shivers moments, that gathering ranks among baseball's best.

When the game started, Martinez pitched himself into the All-Star Game record book by striking out the first four hitters and five overall. "I think it makes it a little more special, being here in Boston," Martinez said after winning the game's MVP award. "Representing the decade, the last one of the century. Being there with all those players around us, I never, never expected it." Said the 80-year-old Williams: "I can only describe it as great. Hell, I haven't had a base hit in 30 years, and I'm a better hitter now than I've ever been in my life."

PEDRO DEFLATES THE INDIANS

GAME FIVE 1999 AMERICAN LEAGUE DIVISION SERIES

Boston fandom quickly discovered many things about the magnificent Pedro Martinez. Likewise, Pedro soon became acclimated with that fandom. Beyond knowing about his fastball, changeup and big-game dominance, fans know Pedro doesn't believe in the so-called Curse of the Bambino. "Maybe they should wake up the Bambino and have him face me and maybe I'll drill him," Martinez once said. No player in Red Sox history lends more credence and meaning to that statement, especially after Martinez's series-clinching performance in Game Five of the 1999 American League Division Series at Cleveland's Jacobs Field.

Martinez suffered a pulled back muscle in the opening game of the series, and the prospects for his return in the playoffs was

dim. After the Red Sox lost the first two games by a combined score of 14-3, it appeared as if the Curse had reared its ugly head again. But when word filtered through Boston that Pedro might be available for the fifth game, the scrappy Sox seemed to hear the buzz and responded with wins in Games Three and Four by a combined score of 32-10. Martinez did not start Game Five, but he went to the mound in the fourth inning with the score tied, 8-8. Pitching six hitless innings, Martinez gave his battle-weary mates just the lift they needed as they scrounged together four more runs to take the game, 12-8, and the series, 3-games-to-2. His teammates carried him off the field in as emotional a display as has ever been broadcast in the history of televised sports.

ROGER CLEMENS' 20-K GAME

APRIL 29, 1986

CLEMENS THREW MOST OF HIS 138 PITCHES IN THE MID-90 MPH RANGE; 97 WERE STRIKES AND ONLY 10 WERE PUT IN PLAY. THE SPARSE CROWD OF 13,414 WITNESSED PERHAPS THE MOST DOMINANT PERFORMANCE EVER BY A PITCHER.

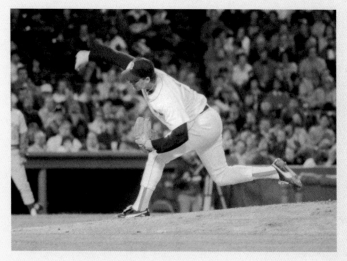

He has done it twice, so in an odd way Roger Clemens took the luster off his own accomplishment by being almost too dominant. But the first time for something always seems more special, and so it was on April 29, 1986 when the Fenway faithful were treated to a pitching performance that had never been seen previously. Clemens had almost unhittable stuff that Tuesday evening as he struck out 20 Seattle Mariners by throwing 70 percent of his pitches for strikes.

The former record for strikeouts in a nine-inning game was 19; Clemens surpassed that number with a ninth-inning K of Phil Bradley. Clemens threw most of his 138 pitches in the mid-90 mph range; 97 were strikes and only 10 were put in play. The sparse crowd of 13,414 witnessed perhaps the most dominant performance ever by a pitcher.

"The people who were here tonight saw history that won't be broken," said Gorman Thomas of the Mariners. "When the last out was made, I wanted to tip my cap. He was that good. It's the finest effort you'll ever see." Said Red Sox manager John McNamara: "I watched perfect games by Catfish Hunter and Mike Witt, but this was the most awesome pitching I've ever seen." Clemens duplicated the feat 10 years later in Detroit on September 18, 1996.

CARL YASTRZEMSKI'S FINAL WEEKEND
OCTOBER 1-2, 1983

THE NUMBERS, AMASSED DURING A GLORIOUSLY COMPETITIVE ERA FOR BASEBALL, WERE PHENOMENAL: 3,419 HITS, 452 HOME RUNS, 1,844 RBIs, AND A 14-GAME WORLD SERIES BATTING AVERAGE OF .352.

Carl Yastrzemski stood in the shadow of the great Wall at Fenway for more than 20 years. That alone makes him royalty from Bangor to Bridgeport and everywhere in between. That he played the game with a hard-nosed style and a purpose in his pose makes the events of October's first weekend in 1983 all the more poignant. "New England, I love you," Yastrzemski said.

It was "Yaz Day" and Fenway was aglow in the celebration of a man who won three batting championships, as well as the MVP award during the "Impossible Dream" season of 1967. When Ted Williams faded away and Yaz came into focus in the early 1960s, the expectations for young Yaz were enormous. By this weekend in the early 1980s, he had surpassed all those expectations. The numbers,

amassed during a gloriously competitive era for baseball, were phenomenal: 3,419 hits, 452 home runs, 1,844 RBIs, and a 14-game World Series batting average of .352.

The cheers on Yaz Day were deafening, not to mention a bit startling because of a deplorable season the Red Sox were enduring. But this wasn't for the team; this was for Yaz. Lasting, fervent applause continued and continued as Yaz was presented with material gifts and heartfelt testimonials. His words were brief and meaningful, but nowhere near as poignant as his lap around Fenway.

"I wanted to show my emotions," he said later. "For 23 years I always blocked everything out. I wanted to show these people that deep down, I was emotional for all that time."

NOMAR GARCIAPARRA'S RETURN

JULY 29, 2001

BEFORE THE DAY WAS OVER, GARCIAPARRA WOULD DELIVER A HOME RUN AND A TWO-RUN SINGLE — THE STUFF OF WHICH LEGENDS ARE MADE.

Folks in New England couldn't decide which happening was more incredible: The injury-riddled Red Sox staying within striking distance of a playoff berth midway through the 2001 season, or shortstop Nomar Garciaparra back in the lineup less than four months after undergoing delicate wrist surgery. On a glorious Sunday afternoon at Fenway Park, Sox fans greeted Garciaparra with a rousing ovation when he stepped into the box for his first at-bat of the season. Before the day was over, Garciaparra would deliver a game-tying home run in the sixth inning and a two-out two-run single in the seventh that won the game, 4-3 — the stuff of which legends are made.

"First game back — homer to straight-away center and a two-out base hit when we needed it. Kind of special," said Red Sox manager Jimy Williams. Added Red Sox pitcher David Cone: "Today gave Boston fans hope — hope that we're gonna give them something special down the stretch." The ever-so-modest Garciaparra said, "It wasn't just me today; it was everybody." But New England knew better; the Red Sox had climbed on Garciaparra's sturdy back and now it was up to him to carry them.

For every Ted Williams or Carl Yastrzemski who graces Fenway Park with a Cooperstown-caliber tool kit, the Red Sox produce a dozen loose screws and wing nuts of assorted shapes and sizes. Free spirits are a staple in team photographs, in grainy black-and-white and in vivid color. They permeate the atmosphere on Yawkey Way, like peanut vendors with operatic pipes.

You can look it up. From Babe Ruth's calorie-busting rookie year in 1914 to Wade Boggs' chicken-fed mysticism 70 seasons later, the Boston organization has assembled a parade of mavericks that the corporate, image-conscious Yankees never could match. Once you have seen Jimmy Piersall flap his arms like a seal or heard the story of Gene Conley trying to hop a flight to Jerusalem after a loss in New York, what Bronx tales can compare? Billy Martin and Reggie Jackson jawing in the dugout with neck veins bulging? Please. In Boston, it's more than permissible to scrap or speak out or stand apart from the crowd. It's a time-honored tradition.

From one decade to the next, through heart-rending finishes and the unyielding fatalism, Boston's oddballs and iconoclasts provided

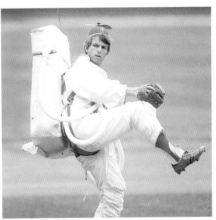

WILLIAM FRANCIS LEE III

comic relief, pathos and great newspaper copy. They made rain delays bearable and the radio talk show telephone lines crackle with sheer outrageousness.

Some were Hall of Fame players; others lived on the fringe of the 25-man roster. Some displayed a pattern of aberrant behavior; others suffered from once-in-a-lifetime brainlock. Some bring a smile to the populace in hindsight; others will be remembered with a trace of sadness or regret. As a collection, they were the kids making faces in the Red Sox team picture.

Exhibit A: William Francis Lee III, who could have carved out a nice, comfortable place in Red Sox lore, instead of the parallel universe he seemingly inhabited, if only he were content to pipe down and change speeds with precision. The art of pitching came naturally

Offbeat characters are as integral to Red Sox tradition as Yankees-hating and second-guessing the manager. They drift on and off stage like the ensemble cast of "Seinfeld." Or in keeping with the Boston theme, "Cheers." There's Dick Stuart as Norm the roguish accountant, and Bernie Carbo as Woody the affable goofball. Sometimes the biggest challenge is keeping all the names and faces straight.

Babe Ruth, the quintessential cleanup man, bats leadoff in this particular order. Before Ruth broke home run

BABE RUTH

barriers and became a national treasure in New York, he was a crude rookie in Boston, so prone to spending money on women and drink that the Red Sox doled out his pay on a daily basis. Rooming with pitcher Ernie Shore as a rookie in 1914, Ruth borrowed his teammate's toothbrush. When Shore informed Ruth of that fact, the Babe replied, "That's all right. I'm not particular."

The 1930s brought intellectual catcher and future spy

MOE BERG

Moe Berg, of whom it was said, "He could speak seven languages and couldn't hit in any of them." Berg played with the Red Sox from 1935 through 1939. He contributed three home runs in that span and raised the collective clubhouse IQ by at least 50 points.

As a promising young outfielder with Boston in the early 1950s, Jimmy Piersall bowed after routine catches, once tormented pitcher Satchel Paige to the point of distraction and fought with everyone from Yankees second baseman Billy Martin to teammate Maury McDermott. Piersall underwent shock treatments at a state

MOE BERG [RIGHT]

MIKE GREENWELL

to Lee, and all the ingredients were in place for him to become his generation's answer to Mel Parnell, a lefty with the guts and gamesmanship to thrive in the unsettling shadow of the Green Monster. But the depth of Lee's perceptions set him apart from the cliche-spewing crowd. Forget his 94-68 record in a Red Sox uniform from 1969 through 1978. At his insightful best, he was more biting than a winter wind off the Charles River and loopier than a maze of rotaries.

In Boston, a city where the snowdrifts will obliterate a Volkswagen, Lee proved a single flake could make a difference. Teammate John Kennedy dropped the "Spaceman" label on Lee early in his career, and it followed him to Montreal, through retirement and into his second incarnation as a Zen Buddhist, Buckminster Fuller-quoting, subsistence farmer off the beaten track in Vermont. More than 20 years after leaving the Red Sox, Lee was traveling to Cuba for baseball exhibitions, catching fly balls behind his back, and dropping the name of Salem witch Lori Cabot into casual conversation. Other than that, he is just your standard retired jock.

HAWK HARRELSON

It was former Brooklyn Dodgers great Duke Snider — we think — who once observed, "Bill Lee doesn't play with a full deck. But the cards he plays, he plays very well."

After the Red Sox sold his friend Bernie Carbo to the Cleveland Indians in 1978, Lee cleared out his locker in anger and bolted for a day. When general manager Haywood Sullivan fined him $533, Lee asked if the fine could be increased to $1,500 so he could take the entire weekend off.

Conversely, Lee was a baseball traditionalist who railed against artificial turf, the designated hitter and efforts to replace Fenway Park. He was an old-school competitor whose penchant for lipping off made others seethe. Lee might be the only player in baseball history who claims to have been sucker-punched by both a teammate (Reggie Smith) and an opponent (Mickey Rivers). Throw in the time Ellie Rodriguez's family attacked him in response to a confrontation in the Puerto Rico winter league, and Lee was 0-for-3.

While Lee's popularity blossomed over 10 years with the Red Sox, Ken "Hawk" Harrelson needed just a summer to put the entire city in

mental hospital in 1952, only to return and play 17 seasons in the big leagues.

Stuart, whose nickname was "Dr. Strangeglove," hit 75 homers and made 53 errors as Boston's first baseman in 1963 and 1964. With his awesome power, outsized ego and awful fielding, he inspired strong reactions pro and con. "Other ballplayers have loyal fans. I have loyal hecklers," Stuart told Sports Illustrated.

Gene Conley, a pitcher with the Red Sox and a forward for the NBA's Boston Celtics, played a starring role in one of the most bizarre incidents in club history. After taking an

JIMMY PIERSALL

early pounding in a 13-3 loss in New York on July 26, 1962, Conley drank several beers in the clubhouse. When Boston's team bus got stuck in traffic to the airport, a hot and agitated Conley hopped off for a bathroom break and took infielder Pumpsie Green with him.

When the traffic suddenly cleared, the two players were left behind in New York City. They dropped by Toots Shor's bar and spent the night at the Commodore Hotel. Green

GENE CONLEY

rejoined the Sox the following night in Washington, where he received a lecture and a $500 fine from manager Mike "Pinky" Higgins. Conley? He bought a plane ticket to Israel, with every intention of visiting the Promised Land. Problem was, he didn't have a passport, so he never made the trip.

Dick Radatz, a portrait in dominance for the Red Sox in the early 1960s, was renowned for striking out Mickey Mantle 47 times in 63 at-bats. After one such confrontation, Mantle unleashed a trail of obscenities and referred to Radatz as a "monster." When the outburst

HAWK HARRELSON

LUIS TIANT

his back pocket. The Red Sox signed Harrelson in 1967 after Kansas City owner Charlie Finley released him for popping off once too often. Harrelson played in 23 games for Boston's Impossible Dream team before busting loose for 35 homers and 109 RBIs in 1968. He quickly became a fan favorite in the guise of the Hawk, his nickname and alter ego.

"Pressure is the biggest killer of performance among athletes and in everyday life," Harrelson says. "That's the way I used to look at it — there was Ken Harrelson, and then there was the Hawk. If I was in the on-deck circle in a big game and there was a man on third base with one out, I'd say to myself, 'Kenny, get out of the Hawk's way and let him go.'"

Harrelson was a walking fashion statement as well as a revelation. His wardrobe won him a spot on America's top 10 best-dressed list. He wore gold medallions and bought a Nehru jacket of every color before they went out of style. In the quintessential act of cool, Harrelson defied old-school tradition and caught fly balls with one hand rather than two. The gesture typically would have infuriated Dick Williams, Boston's

HAWK HARRELSON

crusty manager. But Williams let it slide. "I remember a writer asking why he allowed me to do it," Harrelson says. "Dick told him, 'If he keeps hitting home runs and driving in runs, I don't care what he does.'"

Although Harrelson made $50,000 in salary and even more in endorsements, he rarely paid for anything. In the Boston clubhouse, boxes of shirts and apparel routinely arrived from local clothiers for the Hawk; Harrelson would crack open the boxes and tell his teammates to take what they pleased. His popularity was such that he became one of the first professional athletes to hire a bodyguard for protection. He also retained an elderly gentleman named Wendell as his valet.

Harrelson couldn't muster the heart to say no to autograph seekers, so he would wait in the clubhouse for crowds to dissipate and still came out to find hundreds of fans waiting. He remembers walking into Jimmy's Harborside restaurant after a two-home run game and having the entire place rise en masse to give him a standing ovation.

resonated all the way to the press box, a classic nickname was born.

Radatz, who later became a radio talk show personality in Boston, recalls that a local paper sponsored a contest one summer in which fans were invited to pick a new name for him. "They came up with Smokey the Bear or some damn thing," Radatz says. "I said, 'Is that the best name you can come up with?' I told them we could stay with the Monster, because I had no problem with it. They said, 'We thought you didn't like it.' I told them, 'Nobody ever asked.'"

DICK RADATZ

Luis Tiant, a man with a voice that approximated a Spanish dog whistle, roamed the Red Sox clubhouse from 1971 to 1978. Tiant routinely puffed on a cigar the size of a relay baton, and he dropped a trail of one-liners like a Cuban Johnny Appleseed. He would suck the stogie in the shower and the flame would never go out, a fitting metaphor for his career.

Tiant introduced a herky-jerky throwing motion that became the inspiration for pitchers from Fernando Valenzuela to Nuke LaLoosh. His genius for pitching was his

GEORGE SCOTT

gift, and Red Sox fans applauded from the moment he began his walk from the bullpen.

Tiant was the rare player who knew when to apply the needle to restore equilibrium to a downbeat clubhouse. He would spot a pronounced physical trait in a teammate and pounce, calling Tommy Harper "Liver Lips" and Rico Petrocelli "Pinocchio." The humor wouldn't have resonated so deeply if Tiant didn't back it up with some of the most valiant pitching of his era.

George "Boomer" Scott, the pride of Greenville, Mississippi, sweated off pounds in a rubber suit and wore a

WADE BOGGS   DENNIS "OIL CAN" BOYD   GEORGE "BOOMER" SCOTT   JIMMY PIERSALL

When the Red Sox traded Harrelson to the Indians in 1969 for Sonny Siebert, Vicente Romo and Joe Azcue, enraged fans picketed Fenway Park in protest, and a couple of local companies were sufficiently upset to cancel their season-ticket packages.

Like Harrelson, Dennis Boyd was a child of the South — namely Meridian, Mississippi, a textile and railroad center of 45,000 in the state's eastern hills. His boyhood friend Joe "Paps" Blanks christened him "Oil Can" because of his knack for consuming a heart-stopping brand of moonshine known as "oil."

Oil Can Boyd broke through as a big-time pitcher with Boston in 1985, winning 15 games and working 272 innings. He weighed 152 pounds, he says, with a brick in each pocket. If a pitch were invented, he'd throw it. And if it didn't exist, he'd invent it.

He celebrated strikeouts by pumping a fist in the air, patting teammates on their behinds, and sprinting to the dugout. At his childlike, ebullient best, he provided a refreshing dose of energy and

DENNIS "OIL CAN" BOYD

innocence. "He was flamboyant — sort of like Dennis Rodman," says Mike Easler, a member of the 1984 and 1985 Red Sox teams.

Boyd lacked Rodman's self-serving pretension. When he told stories of his mom and dad, Willie James and Sweetie Boyd, he wasn't lobbying for a movie deal. He spoke from the heart. And while Boston might have found Boyd's routine unsettling, there was more to the Can than a single snapshot could provide. "I'm a historical type person," he says. "I knew about Plymouth and all the small towns. Sometimes I'd go to the symphony."

The Can was beguiling. One night in Cleveland, a fog rolled in so thick the players couldn't see their shoes, much less play baseball. Boyd told reporters, "That's what happens when you build a ballpark on the ocean."

The Can, the Hawk, the Spaceman and the Babe shared a similarly transcendent spirit, if not the same legacy. Their energy was too vibrant to corral and at times too complex to dissect. But the Red Sox were richer for it. And Fenway Park was a heck of a lot of fun when they were there.

BERNIE CARBO

Puka shell necklace that he claimed was made from second basemen's teeth. Scott endeared himself to fans by calling his home runs "taters" and showing cat-like ability at first base. During a tight pennant race, he summarized the sense of urgency by observing that the Yankees "are breathing down our throats."

Bernie Carbo, an outfielder with the Red Sox for five years in the 1970s, once gave an elderly gentleman in the clubhouse $10 to fetch him a cheeseburger and fries, only to later discover the old man was Red Sox owner Tom

Yawkey. Carbo sat his stuffed gorilla, Mighty Joe Young, next to him on team flights. He also took Mighty Joe into the clubhouse and occassionally carried the gorilla to restaurants for breakfast, all in the name of good luck.

During Mike Greenwell's 12 years with the Red Sox, fans sent him stuffed alligators in the mail in recognition of his alleged alligator wrestling. One year Greenwell wrestled with teammate Mo Vaughn during an argument at the

MIKE GREENWELL

batting cage. "I'm a four-wheel-drive pickup type of guy," Greenwell once told reporters. "So is my wife."

Wade Boggs, the poster boy for poultry consumption, made news for his finicky pre-game regimen. Boggs hurt his back taking off a pair of cowboy boots in his hotel room in Toronto, fell out of a vehicle driven by his wife when the passenger door flew open, and claimed to have willed himself invisible when a knife-brandishing mugger menaced him in Florida.